The Babe Signed My Shoe

The Babe Signed My Shoe

By Ernie Harwell
Hall-of-Fame Broadcaster

Edited by Geoff Upward

B ASEBALL AS IT WAS—
AND WILL ALWAYS BE.

T ALES OF THE G RAND O LD G AME

Diamond Communications, Inc.
South Bend, Indiana
1994

The Babe Signed My Shoe

Copyright © 1994 by Ernie Harwell

10 9 8 7 6 5 4 3 2

Manufactured in the United States of America

DIAMOND COMMUNICATIONS, INC.
Post Office Box 88
South Bend, Indiana 46624-0088
(219) 299-9278
FAX (219) 299-9296

Library of Congress Cataloging-in-Publication Data

Harwell, Ernie
    The Babe signed my shoe / by Ernie Harwell ; edited
by Geoff Upward.
        p.   cm.
    Includes index.
    ISBN 0-912083-72-7 : $21.95
    1. Baseball--United States--Anecdotes.   I. Upward,
Geoffrey C., 1950-   . II. Title.
    GV873.H375   1994
    796.357 ' 0973 ' 0207--dc20   94-9249
                                                                        CIP

Dedication

To the four Harwells whose love
and support sustains me:
My sons Bill and Gray and my
daughters Carolyn and Julie.

Special Thanks

To my wife and best friend, Lulu,
my long time inspiration.
To Bill Haney, who first urged me to write a book.
To my hard-working editor, Geoff Upward.
To my patient publishers, Jill and Jim Langford.
To my super typist, Carolyn Raley.

Contents

Foreword ix

Introduction xi

They Also Serve
1 A Day at the Office 1
2 Covering the Bases 15
3 Best Supporting Actors 27

The Players
4 Up For a Cup of Coffee 47
5 Standing the Test of Time 57
6 Trading Places 77
7 Fighting the Good Fight 89
8 Treating 'Em Lightly 103
9 In the Line (Off) Duty 109
10 Out of the Mouths 121

Show Time
11 Another Opener, Another Show 145
12 The Games People Play 151
13 Strange, But (Mostly) True 165

Speaking My Piece
14 Times, They Are a Changin' 185
15 Will Baseball Survive? 199

Afterword
16 Moments in Time 211

Index 217

Chronology: Ernie Harwell

Born Washington, Georgia, January 25, 1918
Atlanta correspondent *The Sporting News*, 1934-1948
Sports Department *Atlanta Constitution*, 1936-1940
Sports Director WSB Atlanta, 1940-1942
Married Lulu Tankersley, August 30, 1941
USMC, 1942-1946
Atlanta Cracker baseball announcer, 1943; 1946-1948
Brooklyn Dodger baseball announcer, 1948-1949
New York Giant baseball announcer, 1950-1953
Baltimore Oriole baseball announcer, 1954-1959
Detroit Tiger baseball announcer, 1960-1991; 1993
CBS Radio Game of the Week, 1992; 1994
Inducted into the Baseball Hall of Fame, August 2, 1981
Tuned to Baseball author, 1985
Diamond Gems author, 1991

Foreword

On August 16, 1990, I visited the home of Ernie and Lulu Harwell in Farmington Hills, Michigan. The purpose of my visit was to shoot a cover story for ESPN's *Major League Baseball Magazine.*

Ernie is a great friend, a great baseball announcer, and an even greater person; and on this day we witnessed one of baseball's great behind-the-scenes moments.

As the camera crew got ready to shoot Ernie's signing of the 1936 magazine story he had written on Wally Moses, Ernie apologized that there might be a telephone interruption. A nurse had just called and asked if Ernie would talk to a teenage boy who was threatening to commit suicide. He wanted to end his life, but he wanted to talk to Ernie first.

Sure enough, the phone rang. Ernie casually walked about 10 feet into the kitchen and answered the phone as if it were just another routine, everyday call. The Voice of the tigers picked up the receiver, and what followed was an extremely poignant conversation that I will never forget.

Ernie's soft, reassuring southern words went something like this:

"Hello...I'm so glad you called. I want you to know that we really care about you. I want you to listen to the broadcast tonight. Paul and I are going to dedicate the pre-game show to you...Please know that the Lord cares about you and loves you. Everything's going to be all right. You're in His hands."

Then a long, hushed pause. I could not believe that I was witnessing this. What could the young man be saying? Ernie tried to respond, but he was having a hard time trying to get a word in. Finally, Ernie found an opening and jumped in with a raised voice:

"No, you're wrong! No!...No, I can't agree!...No!... No, you see, *Trammell* is more valuable than *Fielder*, because he can do so many more things..."

Only in baseball could a teenage boy, planning to end his own life, want to talk to Ernie Harwell first in order to find out who was the Tigers' most valuable player.

And they say that baseball is only a game.

—Warner Fusselle
ESPN's *Major League Baseball Magazine*

Introduction

It was March 1930 in Atlanta. I was 12 years old. The Yankees were playing their way north from spring training. I sneaked down to the front-row box seats at Ponce de Leon Park, and when Babe Ruth came off the field, I begged him for an autograph.

"But kid," he said, "you ain't got no paper. What am I gonna sign?"

"My shoe," I told him. I held my leg over the railing and shoved my foot toward him. I was wearing dirty Keds (the Great Depression equivalent of today's Nikes).

"OK," he laughed. "I'll do it." And, sure enough, he signed my shoe.

The old tennis shoe vanished years ago to wherever old tennis shoes go. But my love for America's game was only beginning.

Four years after my encounter with The Babe I was part of professional baseball reporting—for *The Sporting News*. And after I met and married my treasured wife of 52 years, Lulu, and served four years in the Marine Corps, baseball broadcasting beckoned.

That profession took hold of me and never let go. My seat behind the mike has given me an unobstructed view of the game. From 1948—my first year broadcasting in the major leagues—to 1993, a lot more than just 45 years have passed. I'm not one to talk about the good old days...I think the good days are right now. But I do recognize change. And over the years there have been many changes in baseball.

In 1948 there was no artificial turf—plain old green grass was good enough for everybody. There was no designated hitter—the pitchers did their own batting. We didn't see ballplayers travelling in jeans—they all wore suits and ties, or at least sports coats. Most of the trips were by train, at a leisurely pace—now they fly everywhere.

In 1948 the pay was different. If a player made $15,000,

he was in big money. Now the average pay of a big leaguer is more than $1 million. The lawyers and the agents at that time had not discovered baseball players. There were no mascots—no chickens, birds, or grown men dressed in animal clothes. We saw no ballgirls and no exploding scoreboards.

In the clubhouse in 1948 there was no after-game spread of food for the players...no hair dryers, no personal cellular phones, and no constant music from the stereo. The players couldn't watch themselves on the replays over the clubhouse television set.

If anybody in those days said anything about drugs, you knew he was sick and talking about some kind of medicine. A high-priced steak cost $6 and the fans came to the game to watch the players and not be performers themselves for the TV cameras.

In 1948 Jackie Robinson had just broken the color line, and the few black players in the majors were facing a lot of unwarranted harassment from both fans and players.

There were only 16 major league teams—not 28 like we have today—and the schedule called for only 154 games.

Talk shows hardly existed in 1948, and there was almost no TV. The girlfriends of the players came on trips, but secretly. Now when they travel with the players, the women are not a secret; they even get their pictures in the papers.

Yes, life changes, and baseball with it. The old glory days are surely gone, but each year we add new stories to our great saga—stories of the heroes, the journeymen, the bit players and the supporting cast off the field who help bring this American spectacle to life each summer. It's been a great life for me, and I hope to share a little bit of it with you on these pages. Here's to baseball! And here's to that old tennis shoe, wherever it may be!

They Also Serve…

1

A Day at the Office

"It isn't easy carrying a golf bag around with you on those road trips."—By Saam

My first player interview was a bust.

Still in high school, I had been the Atlanta correspondent for *The Sporting News* for a year and a half. The paper had printed a few of my articles, but my information came from rewrites of the local papers. I had not yet worked up enough nerve to interview any players.

However, in March 1936, I took the plunge. The Philadelphia Athletics came through Atlanta to play the Crackers in a spring exhibition series. The A's had a rookie outfielder named Wally Moses. He hailed from Vidalia, Georgia, and had debuted in 1934 with a .325 average. I contacted *Baseball Magazine* and suggested Moses as the subject for an article. The editor gave me the assignment.

The morning of the first game I phoned Moses at the Georgian Terrace hotel.

"No, I can't see you after the game or tonight," he said. "Come by in the morning and I'll talk with you."

This was a big step for me. I was shy, naive, and really

didn't know what to expect. I was still a hero-worshipper and major league stars were practically gods to me.

I arrived early in the hotel lobby, waited as long as my nerves would permit, and then called Moses' room.

"Yeah," he answered with the enthusiasm of one keeping a dental appointment. "Come on up. I'll talk to you."

When I reached Moses' room, I found him on the bed, talking with his roommate Bob Johnson and Pinky Higgins. He greeted me with a grunt and immediately turned his attention to his teammates. I sat there with pen and note pad, ready to ask the questions I had rehearsed the night before. I don't recall how many I was able to ask. Maybe two or three at the most.

The three players—my heroes—paid no attention to me. They were too involved in a raucous recounting of their sexual conquests of the night before. I got little baseball information; but I did get a quick insight into nighttime ramblings of ballplayers on the loose. There were vivid descriptions of the ladies who entertained them with almost a play-by-play account of their various accomplishments.

Embarrassed and disillusioned, I said a hasty goodbye and went home.

I did write the article. Using a few of Wally's reluctant quotes and a mass of statistics, I managed about 1,500 words. *Baseball Magazine* printed my article in June 1936, and sent me a $10 check. It was the first article I had written for a national magazine. And it was the first time I personally discovered that ballplayers were human beings and not gods.

I never saw Bob Johnson again. Pinky Higgins was always cooperative and friendly when he managed the Boston Red Sox. I travelled with Wally Moses four years (1967-70) when he was a coach with the Tigers, and we became good friends.

We often talked about our Georgia backgrounds, and once I brought him a copy of that *Baseball Magazine* article.

But I never mentioned that he was my first player interview. Maybe the memory—even then—was too painful.

★ ★ ★

As much as my Wally Moses interview changed my perception of ballplayers, a trip to Chicago gave me a new insight into sportswriters.

In mid-boyhood the reality that I was not skilled enough with bat and glove switched my ambition from playing baseball to writing about it. The sportswriters of that era became my idols. I still looked up to the players, but names like Grantland Rice, Westbrook Pegler, Damon Runyan, and Tom Meany were as meaningful to me as Babe Ruth or Rogers Hornsby.

Through studying *The Sporting News* I knew that H.G. Salsinger covered the Tigers, Denman Thompson wrote about the Washington Senators and Ed Burns and Irving Vaughn were Chicago correspondents.

In 1935 my uncle, Lauren Foreman, invited me to visit him in Chicago. I was still in high school, but had been working on the sports desk of the *Atlanta Constitution* for one summer. Knowing that I was going to Chicago, I asked our sports editor, Ralph McGill, for a letter of introduction to the *Chicago Tribune* baseball writers, Ed Burns and Irving Vaughn.

So, letter in hand, I visited the famous Tribune Tower. I entered the sports department and asked for Burns or Vaughn.

"Vaughn's on the road with the White Sox," one of the workers told me. "But Ed Burns is over there with those other guys."

I glanced to the area where the worker had pointed. Burns and the others were jumping around and shouting as they shot a ping-pong ball from an air gun. The ball would bounce off the wall, back to the player, and he would try to catch it in the gun. It was the kind of game you'd expect from 12-year-olds.

I had gone to the famed Tribune Tower expecting sedate and hard-working sportswriters and I got this.

Later, a group of New York writers reaffirmed the same image. The Yankees came to Atlanta for a spring exhibition series at Ponce de Leon Park. As *The Sporting News* correspondent, I was seated in the Cracker office when the writers arrived to interview Cracker president Earl Mann. There were four or five in the group. They had water pistols, party hats, and fake mustaches. They invaded the office and staged a scene worthy of the Marx Brothers.

Later, as a Dodger and Giant broadcaster, I traveled with this same group, and they never seemed that zany. Maybe it was the impressionable days of youth that made them seem so wild. But I learned quickly to be ready for the meeting of the ideal and the real.

★ ★ ★

Baseball and radio have coexisted for more than 70 years. Before these two American institutions came on the scene, fans had only newspapers to depend on for news about their diamond heroes.

Radio coverage of baseball began in the '20s; television emerged in the late '40s and now has taken a dominant position. But there will always be a place for radio and baseball to be together.

My first radio-baseball memory goes back to the 1926 World Series. My older brother, Davis, had a crystal set in our basement in Atlanta. With great pride he would move the little piece of wire called a cat whisker over a dab of mercury and pull in a station from Pittsburgh or some other farther city. There wasn't a loudspeaker—only a pair of earphones. Davis would put one of the phones over his ear and give me the other one. I heard that famous seventh game of the '26 World Series when Grover Alexander fanned Tony Lazzeri in the seventh inning with two outs and the bases loaded, and the Cards went on to beat the Yankees.

From then on I was hooked on radio. In a few years, local stations began to broadcast the Atlanta Cracker games. Our family didn't have a radio then, so I would walk through the neighborhood until I heard the baseball broadcast coming through a window. Then I would camp under that window as long as I could without arousing the suspicions of the household.

The Atlanta announcers didn't travel with the Crackers. When the team was on the road they re-created the game in a studio. This lasted in the minors for many years and is still done in some markets. The major league announcers gave up re-creating in the early 1950s.

The Midwest was far ahead of the eastern cities in baseball broadcasting. In Pittsburgh, on August 5, 1921, Harold Arlin broadcast the first baseball game ever on radio. By the late '20s, Detroit, Chicago, and other cities were covering their teams on a regular basis. Ty Tyson in Detroit had been on the air 11 years before any of the New York clubs aired their games. The Yankees, Dodgers, and Giants had a pact in which they agreed not to broadcast because they felt it would hurt attendance. After Larry MacPhail took over the Dodgers, he broke that agreement in 1939.

Broadcasting is still a big item everywhere. Despite the popularity of TV, radio lives on in cars, on beaches, in shops and homes. Across the landscape of America, in the afternoon, evening, and night, there are and always will be voices on the airwaves bringing baseball to the people who love it.

★ ★ ★

If there is one aspect of baseball life that can drive people into early retirement, it is the travel. They get weary

of the constant wear and tear from flying from city to city
and dragging into hotel lobbies at 3 or 5 A.M.

Two managers who were friends of mine reflected that
general opinion. The late Paul Richards used to tell me: "I
like going to the ballpark and being a part of the game, but
I can't stand the loneliness of a hotel room."

Earl Weaver felt the same way. "It drives me nuts," he
said. "I can't stand the travel."

Sparky Anderson reports to the ballpark around 1:30 in
the afternoon for 7:30 games. Many of the players leave
their soap operas and other TV inducements for an early
arrival at the stadium.

I didn't feel the way they do. I looked at travel as a
chance to see my friends in the major league cities twice a
year. And somebody else was paying for me to stay in modern, well-appointed hotels and eat in famous restaurants.
When I started with the Dodgers in 1948, announcers had
just begun to travel with their teams. So I was on the road as
long as any other announcer, and I always enjoyed it.

Travel in baseball is very important. It may not have
the 80 percent importance rating of pitching, but we all
know that travel is 50 percent of baseball.

Here are some observations, hints, proverbs, definitions, and questions—all personal, just one man's opinions—from my 45 years of big league road games:

• *Proverbs:* Never call home; there is sure to be a crisis…
Never eat at any place called Mom's…The higher the alti-
tude of a restaurant, the worse the food…Quality of a meal
varies inversely with the height of the pepper shaker…
Never change planes in Chicago or Atlanta.

• *Packing hint:* Put all your clothes on one bed. Put all your
money on another. Reduce the clothes by half and double
the amount of money.

• *Questions:* Do maids and housekeepers take college
courses in how to yammer loudly in hotel corridors at 7:30
A.M.? Is there anything dimmer than a hotel room light

bulb? Why do airline ticket agents spend five minutes on a computer when they could write a ticket in half the time? Why are there no real clocks in airports? Who teaches voice training to airline flight attendants?

• *Definitions:* "Catch of the day" is whatever the wholesaler offered to the chef as a good deal..."Garden view" means a room that looks into a light well...An "airline snack" means a pack of 18 salted peanuts.

• *Pet peeves:* Card keys to hotel rooms—you get to your room on the 36th floor, the key doesn't work, and you have to return to the front desk for another...The servi-bar in your room—only $8.50 for a small pack of cashews. I wonder whether the hotel owners realize what a temptation the bar might be to an alcoholic by himself in a lonely room.

• *Travel in the world of literature:* Patrick Dennis quoted two observant employees in his novel *Pink Hotel*. The chef: "Thank God for white cream sauce. It can cover any culinary mediocrity." The telephone operator: "If I don't like a guest, I sock him with a few more phone calls on his bill."

• *Waiter joke:* Customer asks, "Who's gonna win the big game?" Waiter answers, "Sorry, sir, this is not my table."

• *Worst travel scenario:* "Sorry, but we've cancelled your flight."

• *Worst travel scenario No. 2:* "There's a convention at your hotel. It's the National Association of High School Cheerleaders.

• *Worst travel scenario No. 3:* There is heavy construction outside your window...the air hammer tunes up at 6:45 A.M.

• *More questions:* Does anybody ever fill out those suggestion questionnaires? Why do most hotels ignore climatic conditions and set their thermostats according to the calendar? You get heat on a warm winter day and cold air conditioning when it's cool in the spring.

• *Final hints:* Never eat or shoot craps above the ground floor...Never trust a guy who wears his jacket off his shoulder...To ward off pickpockets, wrap your money with a rubber band. Any dip can get into your pocket, but the rubber band creates friction, and the dollar bills can't be removed without your feeling it.

★ ★ ★

The Tigers' first scheduled off-day of the '93 season arrived early—a Tuesday, the day after the night opener in Oakland, California.

Usually, baseball travelers prefer off-days at home. But if there's a road off-day, Oakland is a good place to have it because across the bay is San Francisco, almost everybody's favorite city.

I made no special plans and anticipated an easy, do-nothing kind of off-day. I only scheduled a dinner with coach Dick Tracewski at Mulhern and Schachern's, a great San Francisco restaurant owned by a friend. I invited Tiger announcers Rick Rizzs and Bob Rathbun to join us. Dick was bringing Gene Roof.

Here is a sketchy timetable of the off-day:

• 6:25 A.M.—Radio station calls for short interview.

• 7:05 A.M.—Breakfast at coffee shop.

• 7:50 A.M.—Read article from *Upper Room* magazine and passage from Genesis about Abraham and Isaac.

• 8:10 A.M.—Phone Leo Merta, a friend in Half Moon Bay. He accepts dinner invitation. Will pick us up at 5 p.m.

• 8:40 A.M.—Phone home. Lulu tells me John Lowe's game story made the *Detroit Free Press* despite game's late end. We discuss my "Entertainment Tonight" interview and when it might run.

• 8:50 A.M.—Read two chapters of great new novel *Second Fire* by Robert Wilson, a Tigers fan from Redford.

• 9:00 A.M.—Phone Scott Nickle at Tiger Stadium. He's in meeting and will call back.

• 9:20 A.M.—Phone Gene Myers at *Free Press* to discuss column deadline.

- 10:15 A.M.—Rick Rizzs phones. He and Bob might not join us at dinner. They are going to San Francisco early and might not stay that long.
- 11:30 A.M.—Take 25-minute walk to movie theater. Eat banana and apple on way.
- Noon—Begin watching *Born Yesterday*—alone. Three more people drift in.
- 3:00 P.M.—Walk back to hotel for 20-minute nap.
- 3:30 P.M.—Do stretching exercises in room and jump rope.
- 3:45 P.M.—Scott Nickle phones and reads off list of play-by-play on Ernie Harwell cassette for Tigers April 15 give-away.
- 3:50 P.M.—Watch end of Roy Firestone's "Up Close." *Free Press* columnist Mitch Albom is on.
- 4:00 P.M.—Take warm bath.
- 4:10 P.M.—Dave Newhouse of the *Oakland Tribune* phones. Has written column about our broadcast and wants a tape.
- 4:25 P.M.—A call from lobby. A young man named Tim from Santa Clara says he is an aspiring announcer and wants to talk with me. He visits room and we discuss his career possibilities.
- 5:00 P.M.—Dick, Leo, and I leave for restaurant.
- 5:35 P.M.—We arrive at restaurant.
- 6:00 P.M.—We talk baseball.
- 7:40 P.M.—Ed Moose, who owns nearby restaurant, joins our group. He's a Cardinals fan.
- 8:20 P.M.—Finish great salmon, return to hotel.
- 8:30 P.M.—Watch baseball on ESPN — Toronto at Seattle.
- 8:45 P.M.—Todd Miller of Mayo Smith Society phones to confirm interview with Rick, Bob, and me.
- 9:15 P.M.—Start *San Francisco Chronicle* crossword puzzle.
- 10:20 P.M.—KMPC of Los Angeles calls; I do interview about Tigers.
- 10:30 P.M.—Back to crossword puzzle; 71-across asks: "And —————" Pepys sign-off.

- 10:31 P.M.—I write in answer: "So to bed."
- 10:33 P.M.—I take hint, and so to bed.

★ ★ ★

Baseball announcers are in the business of asking questions. They ask them in their quest for information to use on their broadcasts. And they ask them in interview programs before or after the games.

Yet, there's a turnaround, too. For, indeed, there are a lot of questions posed to announcers. Here are some of those questions—the most frequently asked—along with my answers:

Did you travel with the team?

Yes, I did. I was with them on the plane, in the hotel, on the team bus. Wherever they went, I went. Sometimes it was a grind, but it was much easier than traveling on my own.

Did you ever get tired or bored?

Sometimes tired. Never bored. A stretch of consecutive doubleheaders may have tired me, but I tried to get enough rest to fend off that feeling. I wasn't bored by the games. Even a bad game was different and had some interesting aspect to it.

What's the hardest play to broadcast?

A home run. There's usually doubt about whether the ball is catchable or whether it's a homer. The call requires enthusiasm, but to call a drive a home run and then have it caught is deadly to an announcer. Also, there's often the question of fair or foul in the home run call.

Who paid you, the ball club or the station?

I was paid by the club. But it makes little difference. Any announcer must keep several groups happy. He must please the team, the station, the sponsors, the ad agencies, and the fans. If any of those groups wants him fired strongly enough, he'll be on his way.

How did you get started in broadcasting?
My ambition was to be a sportswriter. I was Atlanta correspondent for *The Sporting News* while I was in high school at the age of 16. Later, I worked six years on the *Atlanta Constitution* while in high school and college. But when I graduated from Emory University, I couldn't find a newspaper job. I auditioned for a sports announcer's spot at WSB-Atlanta and was lucky enough to land the job.
Did you prefer broadcasting on radio or TV?
I enjoyed radio more. On TV the camera is Mr. Big. And the director calls the shot. On radio nothing has happened until the announcer says so. However, the intensity of TV is terrific. I think the ideal for the announcer is to combine the two during a game.
Who is the most exciting player you've ever seen?
Jackie Robinson. My first year in the big leagues was 1948 when Jackie was the Brooklyn Dodgers' second baseman. He could upset the opposition better than any player I ever watched. Jackie was the most competitive player I ever saw and was also the player who got the most out of his abilities.

★ ★ ★

Nothing I've ever done compares with visiting the White House. I've been there four times, and the aura of the place is overwhelming. It is awesome to know that you're standing where the most powerful man in the world rules our government.

On my first visit to the White House, I never got inside—a cause of great embarrassment to one Michigan senator. It happened during the baseball season of 1971. Senator Bob Griffin of Michigan gave a luncheon for the Tigers in the Senate dining room. Eight or 10 players, a couple of Tiger executives, and broadcasters Ray Lane and I attended.

After lunch, the group was invited to the White House to meet President Richard Nixon. Senator Griffin had arranged for the President to greet us. Griffin led us around to the Rose Garden, and our group dutifully waited for the President. After some 20 or 30 minutes, the senator left our group and went into the White House. He returned with an embarrassed look on his face.

"I'm sorry," he said. "The President very much wanted to come out to meet you, but he is working on a very important speech and won't be here. He asked me to send his best."

The Presidential snub frosted the senator. He kept on his best political face throughout the rest of our visit. However, several weeks later each one of us received through the mail a baseball autographed by President Nixon.

In my second White House visit, I not only ventured inside the White House but also got to meet and chat with President Ronald Reagan. And that came as a complete surprise to me.

Dale Petroskey, who was assistant press secretary to the President, arranged the meeting. Dale is one of the founders of the Mayo Smith Society, the leading Tiger fan group.

"Come over from Baltimore," he suggested. "I want to show you around the White House. You'll get to see how a press conference works and meet some of our staff."

I asked Tommy Davis, the Baltimore sports announcer, and Vern Plagenhoff, who covered the Tigers for the Booth chain of Michigan newspapers, to go with me. We arrived early in the morning, went through security at the west gate, and met Dale in the White House.

He showed us around. We met the staff and many of the TV and radio newsmen who covered the White House. I was amazed by the cramped quarters of even the star network TV reporters. Near the end of the tour, Dale called me aside.

"I've a surprise for you. President Reagan is a great

baseball fan, and he wants to meet you. Come with me and wait in the Cabinet Room. We'll get you into the Oval Office in a few minutes."

I waited in that august Cabinet Room until I was summoned. What a thrill to enter the Oval Office. The President greeted me, and we talked about baseball and broadcasting for about 10 minutes. He was most gracious.

There was picture-taking—both video and the still variety. When the time came to leave, I gave the President an autographed copy of my first book, *Tuned to Baseball*. I wrote on the flyleaf, "Best wishes to the President, who was able to overcome being a baseball announcer."

Then President Reagan autographed a copy of my book for me. He later sent me a photo of the two of us in the Oval Office. He wrote on the photo, "From one ole 'teller who' to another. Every good wish and very best regards, Ronald Reagan."

A few months later I was back in the White House— this time with a group of writers and broadcasters. It was during the World Series of 1986. President Reagan staged a luncheon in the Cabinet Room for the writers and announcers who had been inducted into the Baseball Hall of Fame at Cooperstown, New York.

A group of 15 attended, augmented by members of the President's cabinet and staff. When President Reagan entered the room, he looked around and saw a lot of gray hair.

"It's great to be here, playing with kids my own age," he said. We had a lively discussion about baseball broadcasting. The President reminisced about his own broadcasting days for WHO-Des Moines, when he did re-creations of Cubs games.

"It was through baseball that I got into the movies," he recalled. "I had gone to spring training with the Cubs at Catalina Island. Somebody suggested that as long as I was that close to Hollywood, I should take a screen test. I did, and that's how I got into films."

I sat next to Vice President George Bush that afternoon. The ex-Yale first baseman and captain took a good deal of kidding about his baseball career. He seemed as much interested in the game, the writers, and the broadcasters as the President.

Ironically, when Bush began his campaign for President, he used in his campaign literature a picture from this baseball luncheon. The photo showed Bush talking with Mel Allen, Jack Brickhouse, and me. The text said something about business leaders, not acknowledging that this was a lunch for folks who loved baseball.

My fourth White House trip was the most fun of all, because Lulu and my daughter Julie were with me. This visit was part of a full day in Washington. It was October 4, 1991, what we thought at the time was my final year of Tiger broadcasting. Five Michigan members of Congress (Senators Donald Riegle and Carl Levin; Congressmen John Dingel, William Broomfield, and Dale Kildee) headed a group to honor Paul Carey and me with a luncheon in the Russell Senate Caucus Room.

Prior to the luncheon we met with President Bush at the White House. Congressman Broomfield greeted us at the White House and arranged a special private tour. Then, Paul and Nancy Carey, Julie, Lulu, and I went to the Oval Office. We chatted 15 minutes and went through the usual picture-taking.

All of us were impressed by the President's warmth. He also seemed much taller and thinner than he appeared on TV. He gave Paul and me a set of Presidential cuff links and presented the ladies stickpins with the Presidential seal.

We left the Oval Office with that glow only a visit to the White House can bring.

2

Covering the Bases

"If I had my life to live over, I would have liked to have ended up as a sportswriter."—Richard M. Nixon

Sportswriters have always chased the elusive "scoop." Sometimes they land an exclusive story; sometimes they miss it.

This is about a miss. It's a story told to me by the man who made the miss, Harold Parrott. Harold was the first big league traveling secretary I knew. I traveled with him when I broke in with the Brooklyn Dodgers in 1948. Not only was he competent in his job, but he had been an outstanding sportswriter.

Yet, he missed a scoop on Casey Stengel getting the Dodgers' managerial job.

In 1934, Parrott was a boy genius, covering sports for the *Brooklyn Eagle*. All of a sudden he found himself appointed to cover the Brooks' spring training in Miami. There was one drawback. Harold was still living with his mother, who ruled his life with an iron hand. Mother didn't want son Harold to go to Miami and live with those sunburned sinners along the beach.

Parrott enlisted the help of two sportswriters—Tom Meany of the *New York Telegram* and Bill McCullough of the *Brooklyn Times*. Both telephoned Harold's mother and told her that they would watch over him. Besides, they added, all the baseball writers were so busy they never had a chance to drink or carouse.

McCullough also promised that his wife, Gladys, would see that no evil befell Mrs. Parrott's young son.

Gladys McCullough did keep an eye out for Harold. She came looking for him every evening about six o'clock because her husband, Bill, was too drunk to write his story. So Harold had to write not only his own story, but also one for the incapacitated McCullough.

The big story that spring revolved around the Dodgers' manager. Max Carey was soon to be fired. There was much speculation about his successor. McCullough was drinking heavily and couldn't write his stories. Parrott continued to cover for him. Branch Rickey, then with the Cardinals, talked McCullough into a pledge to quit drinking.

A week later, Rickey revisited the Dodgers' camp.

"Bill isn't drinking anymore?" he asked hopefully.

"No, Mr. Rickey," Gladys answered, "But not any less, either."

Big names were being mentioned as the new Dodgers' manager. Parrott would give one the inside track when he wrote his story for the *Eagle*. Later that night when he ghosted for McCullough, he would name some different manager for the *Brooklyn Times*.

Early one morning while still sober, McCullough received a postcard from Glendale, California. The message was: "Leaving for Brooklyn on business." It was signed Casey Stengel. Bill didn't show the postcard to Parrott, and Harold thought it odd that McCullough wrote his own story that night for the first time in more than a week.

McCullough broke the story that Stengel would be named the new Brooklyn manager within a day or two.

He scooped the other 11 Dodgers reporters—including Parrott, who had written most of his stories all spring. It was one of the few stories McCullough wrote all spring, but it was the biggest one of the year in the chronicle of the Dodgers.

Parrott missed the scoop because the man he had befriended finally turned out a story of his own.

★ ★ ★

Sometimes, baseball writers can be tough even on the good guys. Charlie Grimm was always considered one of the most likeable men in all of baseball. During his long career as player, manager, and executive, Charlie always had a smile and a laugh for just about everybody.

But one year—1935—when he was managing the Chicago Cubs, he had a feud going with one particular Chicago sportswriter. If Charlie made mistakes, the writer hopped on him hard. If Charlie did something right, the writer still somehow found fault with him. That season the Cubs were in the pennant race, fighting the Cardinals and the Giants in the final weeks for the National League championship.

Under Charlie Grimm, they became one of the hottest stretch teams in baseball history. They stole the pennant from New York and St. Louis by staging a spectacular drive in September. Grimm's Cubs won 21 straight—a great streak that carried right up to the end of the season and the pennant.

The writer still wouldn't give Grimm credit. After the Cubs lost the next game, he said: "See, Charlie, I knew you couldn't keep it up."

★ ★ ★

There must be a part of any job that every worker dislikes. Maintenance people don't like to do windows, painters would like to skip painting closets, and cooks never look forward to cleaning up after dinner.

Even baseball broadcasting has its dark side. Now,

don't get me wrong, baseball broadcasting is the greatest job in the world. I think all of us who practice the craft agree with that statement. I don't know of any group whose members love their work any more than baseball broadcasters.

However, there is one chore that most of us do not enjoy as much as the other phases of our job. And that's the pre-game show.

Maybe it's because we like doing play-by-play so much. It might be that doing the pre-game interview is a distraction. Or, maybe just the effort to find a guy to talk with is the drawback. Anyway, put it on the record that the pre-game show is the least favorite of all a baseball broadcaster's duties.

Several years ago, two San Diego baseball broadcasters were enjoying a little refreshment in a Chicago lounge. They'd broadcast the Padre-Cub game that afternoon at Wrigley field. The game broadcast had gone well, but the pre-game show had been a disaster. The mike kicked out at the opening, and the Cub star to be interviewed didn't show up because some sweet young thing caught his attention about the time he was due to report for the interview.

So the two announcers were trying to relax and forget about their travails earlier in the day.

A rather attractive lady sauntered over toward them. "Hello, gentlemen," she said. "Can I join you?"

"Please do."

It didn't take her long to get to the point. "Gentlemen," she said, "I'll do anything for $100."

The two announcers looked at each other. Right away, in unison, they said, "How about the pre-game show?"

★ ★ ★

There are all kinds of ways to break into major league baseball broadcasting. One of the most unusual debuts was that of Greg Wyatt, who became a TV sports star for Fox Television.

In 1964, the California Angels played their home games at Dodger Stadium. There was a lot of room in the press area, and Angels management allowed ambitious would-be student announcers to practice announcing into a tape machine. One of these young tyros was Greg Wyatt. Often before a game, I had some long and interesting talks with Greg about his ambitions and our profession.

I write this to set the scene for Wyatt's debut, which came Sunday afternoon, August 30, 1964, when the Tigers were playing the Angels at Dodger Stadium.

That Sunday in 1964 marked my wedding anniversary. The Tigers' next series was in Chicago. I'd arranged for my wife, Lulu, to meet me that Sunday evening in Chicago.

For me to reach Chicago that evening, I had to catch a 6 P.M. plane out of the Los Angeles airport. It was going to be a close call. It became even closer when my broadcast partner, Bob Scheffing, had to miss that game to attend the funeral of his father-in-law. That meant I would have to remain after the game and announce the scoreboard show. The game dragged on. With each agonizing delay it seemed more likely I'd miss my plane and my anniversary evening. Finally the game limped to a conclusion. I was now pressed for time.

If I broadcast that post-game show, I was certain to miss my plane. While the final commercial was on, I bolted out of the booth and found young Greg Wyatt.

"How would you like to make your big league debut?" I asked.

"Great. Sure," he answered. "But how?"

"You'll do the scoreboard show," I told him. "Read the National League scores, then the American. You'll do great."

"I'll try," he said.

He did. He entered the booth as I left it. He sat down and started the show.

I rushed out of the stadium, grabbed a ride to the airport, and caught my plane. That night Lulu and I celebrated our anniversary in Chicago—thanks to Greg Wyatt.

The youngster made his debut that Sunday afternoon. I never heard any more about the scoreboard show. The Tigers and WJR never mentioned it. And there was no reaction from any of the listeners.

I appreciated Greg Wyatt's taking over the show. He gave me a chance to reach Chicago for my anniversary celebration. And he got the chance to make his big league announcing debut and prove to himself that he was good enough to make the grade.

★ ★ ★

Maury Povich hasn't always been the host of a hard-hitting TV show. He had to start somewhere. That somewhere was Washington, as a gopher for baseball announcer Bob Wolff. Maury's ambition was to replace Wolff someday as the voice of the Washington Senators.

Maury's dad was Shirley Povich, longtime Washington baseball writer. The game was in Maury's blood and he enjoyed being what he called "an associate producer." During his college days he would travel with the Senators in the summer and work with Wolff.

Once in 1960, Wolff had to leave his broadcast of a Washington-Detroit game at Tiger Stadium to fulfill an assignment in New York. He turned the microphone over to young Maury. It was the first time Povich had ever done any play-by-play.

As Povich was describing the game, up to the plate stepped the Senators' slugger, Harmon Killebrew. Harmon took his best swing and launched a drive deep into the left-field upper deck. The rookie announcer gave the blow a fully descriptive call and then added: "In all my broadcasting career, that's the longest home run I've ever seen." Baseball gets many people started. Some day, I may reveal how Mrs. Field, the famous cookie lady, was once a ball girl in Oakland; how Dan Rather was the public-address announcer for the Houston Astros before he became a famous TV news anchor; and how Rush Limbaugh, the radio talk show host, was a runner for me during a playoff series in Kansas City.

★ ★ ★

Jon Miller is at the top of his profession. He is ESPN's No. 1 baseball announcer and the much-respected voice of the Baltimore Orioles.

It was different for Jon 20 years ago. He was a down-and-out, unemployed TV sports anchor. Jon, at 22, had an impressive résumé of broadcasting football, basketball, hockey, soccer, and horse and auto races. But his career came to a screeching halt.

Then, a last-minute break came his way — just in time. His Santa Rosa, California, TV station had gone broke. Looking for a broadcast partner, Monte Moore, the Oakland A's announcer, had struggled through hundreds of tapes. He came across one from Jon Miller. He liked it. With the approval of owner Charlie Finley, Monte picked Miller as his new partner, and Jon was on his way.

"I'd never heard of the guy," Monte remembered. "But he had a good, fresh sound—better than all the others. I had heard hundreds of tapes when I got to his. I almost didn't listen, but I told myself I owed it to this unknown. So I gave it a shot."

In 1974, Miller became Monte's partner. He was a success. But the volatile Finley entered the scene, and Jon was gone after one year. At the Chicago baseball writers' dinner, Finley met Bob Waller, who had announced for the

White Sox. Impulsively, he offered Waller Jon's job, insisting on an immediate answer.

"If you don't say 'yes' right here at the banquet, I'm not giving you the job," he told Waller. Waller accepted, and Miller was out on the street again.

He was out of baseball for the next three years. Then Monte Moore became part of his life again. The Texas Rangers, looking for a new announcer, contacted Monte. He turned down the job, but recommended his one-time partner, Jon Miller. Jon landed the job and worked for the Rangers for two years. He moved to the Red Sox and spent three seasons in the Boston booth before joining the Orioles' broadcast team in 1983.

It was in Boston that Miller's career began to take off. He worked with the veteran Ken Coleman, who loved to make use of Jon's originality and versatility. During rainouts or slow spots in the game Ken would urge Jon to do imitations and impressions of other announcers. That led to a demand for Miller on the banquet circuit and eventually to network baseball assignments. He first received national exposure on NBC for four years, and for the last several seasons has been the big gun for ESPN on Sunday night baseball.

"It was Ken Coleman who gave my career its needed boost," Jon says. "He recognized my unique talent and helped me to make the most of it."

Jon Miller is on top now. But he can thank two veteran announcers for his success—Monte Moore, who twice befriended him, and Ken Coleman, who recognized that Jon's unique style demanded national attention.

★ ★ ★

Thirty-three Girl Scout cookies almost kept Rick Rizzs out of the big leagues.

Rick is now the highly regarded voice of the Tigers, the

top of his profession, but he almost didn't make it to the majors. The story goes back to late January 1983. Rizzs had worked his way through the lower minors into the Columbus, Ohio, play-by-play job. One more step, and he would be a major leaguer.

Rick sent broadcast tapes to Cleveland, San Diego, the two Chicago teams, and Seattle. Melody Tucker, director of broadcasting at Seattle, phoned him.

"You're in the finals here, Rick," she said. "Our Mariners owner, George Argyros, wants you to meet him for an interview in Newport Beach, California. If he likes you, the job is yours."

Finally, after 10 years of broadcasting in Carbondale, Illinois; Alexandria, Louisiana; Amarillo, Texas; and Columbus, Rick had his big chance.

Rizzs was scheduled to meet Argyros on Wednesday in Newport Beach, but on Monday he competed in a Girl Scout cookie-eating contest with 12 other Columbus celebrities. In three minutes, he ate 33 cookies and finished third.

Rick reported to his radio station, WBNS, at five the next morning and broadcast his sports show at six. However, by seven, he began to feel excruciating pains in his chest. He was certain it was a heart attack. He met his doctor at the hospital, where he underwent an EKG and various blood tests. The doctor insisted that he spend that Tuesday night in the hospital.

While hooked up on tubes in the emergency room, Rizzs telephoned Melody Tucker in Seattle. He envisioned his big league chances slipping away.

"I can't get to California for my Wednesday interview," he told Melody, "because they think I may be having a heart attack."

"Mr. Argyros is leaving Friday for a two-week vacation to Greece," she said. "Can you make it here by Friday?"

"I'll be there," Rizzs told her.

The doctors were still not certain if he'd had a heart attack or not. They tried to keep him in the hospital for further tests. But this was his real chance at the big leagues, so he talked them into letting him fly to Newport Beach. Rizzs flew to Newport Beach and met with Argyros for an hour. He explained to him how nervous he was—nervous about the job and nervous about his chest pains. His story about eating those cookies broke the ice. Argyros laughed about it, and Rizzs relaxed—somewhat. Finally, Argyros reached across the table, shook his hand, and said: "Welcome aboard. Any man who won't let 33 Girl Scout cookies, and severe chest pains stop him deserves to be a big league announcer."

"I found out later I really didn't have a heart attack," Rick recalls. "What happened was this: When I ate all those cookies, my sternum underwent tremendous pressure and that pressure caused all my pain."

Those 33 Girl Scout cookies almost stopped Rizzs' big-league career—before it started.

★ ★ ★

Radio engineer Howard Stitzel has been part of Tigers baseball since 1948. When Howard turned his first knob for a Tigers broadcast, Harry Heilmann was still announcing, and such stalwarts as Hal Newhouser, George Kell, Virgil Trucks, and Vic Wertz were challenging the New York Yankees' dynasty.

Since then, Howard has served a full roster of Tigers broadcasters. He has given a million cues, eaten thousands of free meals in America's pressrooms, and sneaked hundreds of baseballs into his socks.

"A couple of years ago," Stitzel recalls, "I ran into this guy at the airport. He came over and said: 'You don't remember me, but 20 years ago when I was a youngster you gave me a baseball, and I want to thank you for it.' We talked a little longer, and I found out this guy was the president of Delta Airlines."

Stitzel is in fine shape at age 77. Though he eats enough for three people, he never gains weight. "The most desserts I had at one meal," he said with a grin, "was on one of our Tiger charter trips when I ate seven or eight pies. But they were small."

The way Stitzel landed his Tiger job was almost too easy. He had served in World War II as a Navy radio operator. After his discharge in November 1945, he found a job at radio station WKAP in Allentown, Pennsylvania, before coming to Detroit.

Stitzel had no contacts here, but in the spring of 1948 he applied for jobs at WJBK, WXYZ, WWJ, and WJR. The next day, he received a call from Don Hein, the supervisor of engineering at WJBK.

"I've been overloaded with my studio work and my job with the Tiger broadcasts," Don told him. "I want you to be Harry Heilmann's engineer."

Stitzel worked with Harry until the announcer died in 1951. Harry did not travel with the team, but did re-creations of the road games from the Telenews Theatre on Woodward Avenue. Fans would gather there every day to watch Heilmann broadcast and Stitzel turn the knobs.

Stitzel's Tiger career was interrupted in the early 1970s, when WJR decided not to use an engineer. So Paul Carey and I worked without Stitz for 16 years until 1991, our last year together.

Now he is back in the booth with Rick Rizzs and Bob Rathbun. Through his career, Stitzel worked with Heilmann, Ty Tyson, Paul Williams, Van Patrick, Dizzy Trout, Mel Ott, Kell, Bob Scheffing, Gene Osborn, Ray Lane, Carey, and yours truly.

Stitzel grew up on a farm in Fleetwood, Pennsylvania, and maintains a love for plants and flowers. He is proud of the magnificent garden at his Southgate home. Stitzel is also proud of his Tigers engineering career and his 1968 World Series ring. He is hoping for another before he retires.

3

Best Supporting Actors

"I've had a life long ambition to be a professional baseball player, but nobody would sign me."—Gerald R. Ford

Sometimes you don't have to be a player to make an impact on the game—even in the role of a baseball pioneer. For more than 40 years, Francis Carter Bancroft was associated with baseball—either as a player, manager, or an executive. Talk about going back a ways: He went all the way back to the American Civil War. While serving with the Union, he organized baseball games among the soldiers.

After his army service, Bancroft did many things. He founded a hotel (the Bancroft House) in New Bedford, Massachusetts; owned a theater and opera companies; and managed a hockey team for several years.

When baseball's first minor league, the International League, was formed in 1878, New Bedford entered a team. Well, Mr. Bancroft was the manager of that New Bedford team and made quite a success out of the job. The next two years he managed at Worcester, and it was during one of those off-seasons that Bancroft led his team on a tour of Cuba and introduced baseball to the people of that island.

He went to Detroit and managed the Detroit Wolverines in 1881, their first year in the National League. He stayed in Detroit only two years and then moved along again.

In fact, Bancroft was always moving along. He became baseball's "movingest" manager, piloting seven different teams in the major leagues. After his managing days were over, Bancroft went to the front office. He worked for 29 straight years as business manager of the Cincinnati Reds. During that time he made his second trip to Cuba and also took another journey to Hawaii. He has long been known as the "Father of Cuban Baseball."

Bancroft was quite a force in those early days of baseball history, but he reached the pinnacle of his career in 1884. That season he managed the Providence Grays and had on his staff one of baseball's most famous pitchers, Charles Radbourn. Old Hoss Radbourn won 60 games that season with a 1.38 ERA, and Bancroft's Providence team won the National League pennant by $10\frac{1}{2}$ games. They met the New York Metropolitans in the World Series and beat them in three straight games.

Francis Carter Bancroft, the Father of Cuban Baseball, never played, but he was a major influence on the game during his 40-year association.

★ ★ ★

The baseball commissioner's office has not been without drama and controversy over the past several years. In fact, the job and the men who have served in it have had a colorful history from the outset.

Baseball's first commissioner was Federal Judge Kenesaw Mountain Landis—who epitomizes the kind of man the owners seek when the job has to be filled.

Before Landis, baseball was ruled for 17 years by a three-man commission—the two league presidents and Cincinnati owner Garry Herrmann.

However, around the time of World War I, dissatisfaction with the three-man rule developed. Then came the Black Sox scandal of 1919-20, bringing the matter to a head. Several months after the Black Sox scandal broke, Herrmann resigned and baseball was then governed by John Heydler, president of the National League, and the American League president Ban Johnson. These two could never agree on issues, and the game went along in a state of unrest.

The Black Sox scandal precipitated final action. Two of the owners of the Yankees wanted to break from the American League. The White Sox and Red Sox were willing to join them. So, in a meeting in Chicago in 1920, the old National League disbanded itself, and the eight clubs that had been in the National League added the Yankees, White Sox, and Red Sox, to organize a new league, which they called the National-American League. They then awarded a 12th franchise to Detroit, which still had the Tigers in the old American League.

The league voted to put into effect a three-man ruling committee composed of men outside of baseball—the chairmanship going to Judge Landis, who would be the supreme ruler of all leagues joining in the plan.

American League president Ban Johnson, by then losing his once-great power and believing the National League 12-club setup was merely a bluff, put up a struggle.

However, owners in both leagues began to see the folly of their fighting. Frank Navin of Detroit and Herrmann of the National League were the leading peacemakers. The owners agreed to meet together and forget about the baseball war.

They met November 12, 1920, in Chicago, and it was then that Judge Landis was named as baseball's first commissioner. The 12-club National-American League was dead. It had lived for only 48 hours.

The owners voted to hand Landis the big job. At first, he refused. Then after further conversation, Landis agreed to accept if he were given absolute control over baseball. Baseball had a one-man ruler, a man with complete power over the game.

Landis' title was first the "Director-General of Baseball." The office might have carried that title even today, except that the old judge thought that such a title was a bit too fancy. "That sounds too highfalutin," he said. "Let's just make it Commissioner."

So, commissioner it has been.

★　★　★

Charlie Martin was the ideal subject to point out the difference in the operation of a baseball team then and now.

I interviewed Charlie in early 1992. When he died the following year at the age of 100, he was the oldest former baseball executive.

Martin worked for the Tigers from 1923 to 1958. He was ticket manager, stadium superintendent, and traveling secretary. It was through the theater business that Charlie became part of the baseball business. He managed the old Michigan Theater at the corner of Michigan Avenue and Washington Boulevard. Mrs. Frank Navin, the wife of the Tigers' president, often attended Wednesday and Saturday matinees there.

"Why don't you drop by and see my husband at the ballpark?" Mrs. Navin asked Martin. "He is thinking about setting up a ticket agency for the Tigers, and I told him about you."

Navin hired Martin. He set up an agency at Fonds' drugstore in downtown Detroit.

Until then, the Tigers never had sold tickets in advance. You bought a ticket the day of the game, or—at best—you could buy a ticket at the park for the next day's game after the fifth inning of the ongoing game.

Martin enjoyed working for Navin.

"He was a warm and friendly man," Charlie remembered. "Walter O. Briggs was a good boss, too, but he was a man of moods and could be very tough at times."

One afternoon, Mrs. Martin drove to Navin Field to pick up her husband. She parked on the street in front of the ballpark. Navin was walking by and saw Mrs. Martin. "Don't sit here waiting for Charlie," he said. "Come on up to the office and see how busy your husband is."

Mrs. Martin accompanied Navin to the offices. Navin opened the door, and the two of them saw the "busy" Martin playing cards with his coworkers.

Besides Navin, Charlie Martin had two close friends in Charlie Gehringer and Hank Greenberg. The stars often dropped by the ticket office and chatted with Martin. Gehringer later became general manager of the club while Martin was with the Tigers. Greenberg remained Martin's lifetime friend and even helped him land a job in Lakeland, Florida.

Charlie was stadium superintendent for 11 years. He enjoyed that job less than his ticket managership, but liked it more than the traveling secretary assignment. He was suddenly named traveling secretary in mid-season of 1949.

Briggs called Charlie into his office. "Charlie," he said, "you're our new traveling secretary. I'm firing Clair Berry. You will have to go to Boston and replace him."

"It was the toughest thing I ever did," Martin said. He kept the job for three years and then concentrated again on the ticket department.

Tickets had been Charlie's business almost all his life. He was born in Chicago, but his family moved to Grand Rapids when he was five years old. He enlisted in the Army in 1917 and became a bugle boy in World War I. That trusty bugle sat for years on the window in his Royal Oak, Michigan, apartment.

After the war he returned to Grand Rapids and got a job selling tickets at the Majestic Theater. The theater transferred him to Cleveland, where he also sold tickets. Then in 1920, he came to Detroit to work at the Michigan Theater, where chance and circumstance led to his career as Tigers ticket man.

★ ★ ★

He was a 13-year-old towhead, living in Corktown, a neighborhood in Detroit near the ballpark, with his mom and grandparents. He was the smallest kid for his age in the neighborhood, but the bigger kids let him tag along when they swept out Briggs Stadium after games.

Then one day he met Hank Greenberg. The big Tigers first baseman said: "Whitey, meet me tomorrow morning at 10:00. I'm taking extra batting practice, and I want you to shag the flies." That was Charles Frederick Collins' real introduction to the world of baseball. For the next 60 years, he was part of that world, retiring at 73 as custodian of the visitors' clubhouse at Tiger Stadium.

Charles Frederick Collins isn't Whitey anymore. He's Rip now. In those boyhood days, Rip used to walk out of the park with Greenberg. "Hank got to know my grandmother," Rip said. "He'd walk all the way to our house and then take a cab home. Sometimes, he'd sit and talk with my grandmother. She was the first one to call him 'Hankus Pankus.'"

Greenberg gave his first baseman's mitt to young Whitey. Fifty years later when Hank returned for ceremonies to retire his uniform, he autographed the mitt.

Hank helped Collins get a job as visitors' batboy and clubhouse man, a position he held from 1933 to 1936. He knew the day's diamond idols—Babe Ruth, Lou Gehrig, Jimmy Foxx, and Lefty Grove.

"Funny thing about The Babe," he recalled. "He wouldn't autograph anything but a baseball. *(Well, almost anything. He did sign something else for me, which I talk about in the Introduction.)* He was always suspicious of someone forging his signature on a letter or contract."

Collins enlisted in the Marines. He went to boot training at Parris Island, and later sailed the North Atlantic as an admiral's orderly. Rip requested transfer to Air Naval Training at Chapel Hill, North Carolina. From there he went to Pensacola, Florida, to become a flight instructor. He used his old Hank Greenberg mitt and played first base on the same Marine team with Ted Williams, who gave him his nickname of Rip.

After the war, Collins was a Detroit fireman for six years. He reenlisted for the Korean conflict. As a fighter pilot he flew 109 missions, and won two Distinguished Flying Crosses and eight air medals.

On his return to civilian life, Collins became assistant to LeRoy "Friday" Macklem, the Lions' equipment manager. He switched to head equipment man for the Wheels. When they folded, Rip landed his job as the Tigers visitors' clubhouse man.

After 18 years of watching modern stars, Collins wasn't impressed. He had seen The Babe and Gehrig, so the current millionaires were just customers. In Korea, he watched men die and he knows what a real hero is.

What does impress Rip is warmth, generosity, and friendship. He saw Dwight Evans send his wife to tend to teammate Fred Lynn's ailing wife. He watched the Angels' Frank Tanana befriend a rookie who was insulted and abused by veteran players. He had a great career and was respected as one of baseball's supporting cast.

★ ★ ★

Jim Schmakel's career in baseball started in 1965 with 50 words or less.

Now, 28 years later, he is an integral part of the Detroit Tigers' day-to-day operation. In the Tigers' media guide,

Schmakel is listed as "assistant director of equipment." Translation: He's manager of the Tigers' clubhouse.

Players spend more time in their clubhouse than at home. Jim is invaluable in supplying equipment, comfortable surroundings, and solid meals.

"We couldn't do without Jim," Alan Trammell said. "In his quiet, efficient way, he gets the job done and is a great help to all of us."

While growing up in Toledo, Schmakel was a Yankees fan. When the Mud Hens returned to professional baseball after a 13-year absence, Jim was thrilled. He entered a batboy contest that first Mud Hens year (1965), and his 50-words-or-less essay on "Why I want to be the Mud Hens Batboy" finished third.

"The first two winners became batboys," Jim recalled. "I won a season pass and saw every Mud Hens game."

He entered the contest again in 1966 and won.

"Scott Brady (now a Coldwater, Michigan, dentist) was the other winner," Schmakel remembered. "Scott became the visiting batboy, and I was batboy for the Mud Hens."

Jim graduated from batboy—at $1 a week—to clubhouse worker at $10 per week in 1967, and held that job until 1974. He then became the visitors' clubhouse manager.

Meanwhile, he had become a teacher and also coached basketball at Woodmere High School and the University of Toledo. In 1978 he took a traveling job in the business world, but couldn't forget his baseball connections.

"That May of 1978," Jim remembered, "I read in the paper that Pio DiSalvo had become the Tigers' equipment manager." Jim gave him a phone call just to say hello.

"Yeah," Pio told him, "they gave me this job, but I hate it. I'd rather go back to being a trainer in the minors." That September, DiSalvo returned to Toledo, and Schmakel became the Tigers' equipment man.

As a former coach and teacher, Jim has kept his link to education through the batboys who work with him. He emphasizes the importance of schooling.

"To be a Tiger batboy," Jim says, "a youngster must be at least 16. He must be an honor-roll student, and his high school must enter a cooperative agreement with the Tigers' organization."

Seventy young men have worked for Jim, and 98 percent have gone to college. His first worker, John Nelson, is manager of the visitors' clubhouse at Tiger Stadium. Others are successes in the world of business. Matt Good is a banker in Cincinnati. Dave Cowart and Bob Mical are with Detroit engineering firms. Carl Dobronski is a schoolteacher, and Eric Pytlak is a meteorologist at the Cincinnati airport.

The effort and dedication of the clubhouse boys inspired Dave Bergman and other Tigers to set up a scholarship for Schmakel's workers. Last year, the fund awarded $7,000 toward college educations. The directors of the fund—along with Bergman and Schmakel—are Trammell, Mike Henneman, Travis Fryman, Cecil Fielder, and Mickey Tettleton.

Schmakel lives in Perrysburg, Ohio, with his wife, Pat. They have three youngsters—Katrina, 15; Bryan, 13; and Jay, 7. Jim is with them when the Tigers are on the road, but his home games present a whole different schedule for the family.

For a night game, Schmakel leaves home at 9 A.M. He drops off the kids at school, shops for groceries, and drives 70 miles to Tiger Stadium. When the game is over, Jim and his crew work another two and a half hours. He drives home, arriving at 2:30 or 3 in the morning. If a day game follows a night game, Jim and the batboys sleep in the clubhouse.

"I have a great job," Schmakel said. "I love it."

★ ★ ★

Frank Feneck grew up in the shadow of Briggs Stadium and dreamed of playing in the major leagues. He didn't make it as a player, but he has been a very important part of the Tigers' scene. And he has lasted much longer in his job than he would have by fielding grounders or swinging for the fences.

Frank is the chief groundskeeper at Tiger Stadium. The official description of his job is assistant director-stadium operations.

"I grew up in Corktown," Feneck recalls. "We lived right near the ballpark until the Lodge Expressway came along and destroyed our house and most of the neighborhood."

Feneck went to Franklin School. When classes were over, he would race to the ballpark to see the last three innings of every game. He later played second base at Western High School, three-time city champions. The Indians and Cubs scouted Frank, but he had his eye on the Tigers.

"When the Tiger scout, Ray Meyer, passed me over for Ronnie Rozman, a Catholic Central pitcher, I gave up," Feneck remembers. "I enlisted in the Navy at 17 and stayed in the service for four years."

Feneck continued to play baseball in the Navy, and because the players had to help maintain the fields, he laid a foundation for groundskeeping that would help him in his career.

After naval duty, Feneck returned to Detroit and went into construction work. He had friends on the Briggs Stadium grounds crew and would often visit them. Tony Kochivar, the head groundskeeper, approached Frank one afternoon.

"How would you like to work here?" Kochivar said.

Frank jumped at the chance. Construction business was slow, and he liked the idea of working outdoors. He started to work in May of 1963. The pay was $2.85 an hour when Frank started. He had to take a cut. But Frank feels he has been well rewarded over the years.

"I love it," he said. "It's been fun, and I have a chance to work with some really interesting people."

Different Tiger managers had different ideas about groundskeeping. Charlie Dressen had little interest in the condition of the field. Mayo Smith, who managed the champions of 1968, complained to Feneck about the heavy grass during the 1969 season. "Wait a minute, Mayo," Feneck told him. "The grass was exactly the way it was in 1968. The difference is, your team's not winning this season."

When Billy Martin managed the Tigers, he asked Feneck to pile dirt around first base to slow the fast runners on the Cleveland and Baltimore teams.

"Rocky Colavito was coaching at first for the Indians," Feneck remembers. "And he kept busy trying to smooth down that extra dirt."

Some players have enlisted the help of Feneck. Former Tiger Rusty Staub was one who was hard to please. Staub continually complained about the high grass. Also, he had a problem with noise from an electric fan in the clubhouse.

"Rusty liked to take a nap in the clubhouse," Feneck said. "And the noise from the fan kept him awake. Our guys oiled the fan and got rid of the noise. After that, Rusty said he missed the hum of the fan and couldn't sleep without it."

A couple of years ago Frank got into an argument with Red Sox manager John McNamara and his third baseman, Wade Boggs. It started when McNamara told Frank the bag at third was inside the foul line. Boggs, defending Frank, pointed out to his manager that the bag was in the correct place. Then Boggs started in another direction.

"The bag's OK," he said, "but your home plate is cockeyed...cockeyed by the width of my thumb."

"You're wrong, Wade," Feneck replied. "If the plate was off, those foul lines wouldn't line up perfectly the way they do."

That discussion was mild compared to the outbreak between Feneck and Texas manager Bobby Valentine. Valentine had complained to plate umpire Joe Brinkman about excess dirt in front of home. Brinkman called Frank to the plate during the national anthem. The three stood there and a heated discussion began.

"What's the matter here?" Valentine said. "Why so much dirt in front of home plate?"

"The players did that during batting practice," Feneck answered.

"Is the rest of the field that way?" Valentine demanded.

"It's the same way," Feneck said.

"You're a liar!" Valentine shouted.

Now the argument was really hot. The two almost came to blows. But Brinkman intervened, the national anthem finished, and the game started.

If it wasn't a player or a manager, Feneck had to contend with the weather.

"The toughest time I ever had," he recalled, "was on April 6, 1982. The Toronto Blue Jays came in for the opener and we had 10 inches of snow on the field.

"The day before the opener we tried to get the snow off the tarp. It was impossible. We had punctured the tarp. We couldn't remove the snow. Both games of the opening series had to be postponed."

It was just another incident in the life of a top-notch groundskeeper.

But Frank Feneck loves his job. He's happy that he made it to Tiger Stadium—even if it wasn't as a player.

★ ★ ★

Hooray for Cooperstown! The Hall of Fame in that quaint little town is finally recognizing baseball scouts. A special exhibit of photographs and artifacts associated with scouting was unveiled in 1993. Six outstanding scouts were recognized as features of this first exhibition.

Wish Eagan, who scouted for the Tigers for 40 years,

was one of these honorees. Wish signed Hall-of-Famers Hal Newhouser and Hank Greenberg. Egan was a close friend and confidant of Detroit owner Frank Navin, and directed Billy Pierce, Dizzy Trout, and Hoot Evers to the Tigers.

Another scout recognized in Cooperstown was Joe Cambria. Joe specialized in finding talent for the Washington Senators in Cuba, Mexico, and Latin American countries. One of his scouting reports on a Cuban pitcher read, "Lots of enthusiasm, not much of an arm. Suggest he go into another business." That was Cambria's report on Fidel Castro.

Howie Haak is still an active scout and for 35 years has been known as the "King of the Caribbean." He has worked for the Cardinals and Pirates and is now on the staff of the Houston Astros. Howie's No. 1 contribution was signing Hall-of-Famer Roberto Clemente.

Another scout honored at Cooperstown was Paul Krichell, who signed Lou Gehrig for $1,500 and discovered Whitey Ford, Phil Rizzuto, Leo Durocher, and Tony Lazzeri.

The other two scouts featured in the Cooperstown exhibition were Bobby Mattick and Cy Slapnicka. Mattick has been in baseball 60 years as an outfielder, scout, and big league manager. His scouting resume lists the signings of Frank Robinson, Vada Pinson, Don Baylor, Rusty Staub, and Curt Flood.

Slapnicka signed more than 30 major leaguers but will best be remembered as the one who discovered Bob Feller. He watched Feller pitch on a semi-pro diamond outside of Des Moines, Iowa, and knew right away that Feller was destined to be a superstar.

It's great to see Cooperstown honor these men who have made a real contribution to the game. All of them have had an ability to recognize potential greatness in the talent they have scouted. Where would baseball be without these men who discovered the stars?

★ ★ ★

In these days of big money in baseball, it's ironic that the most unappreciated and lowest-paid people in the game are the most important.

I'm talking about the big league coaches. They work harder than anybody, and they are paid less than most. There is no minimum for a coach's salary. He will be paid what the team wants to pay him. Many of the coaches stay in the game not because of their salaries, but to remain in the Major League Baseball pension plan. It is a lucrative plan and makes continuing their careers worthwhile.

In the early days of baseball, the coach was generally a friend and drinking buddy of the manager. There was one, maybe two coaches on each team. Until a fellow named Arlie Latham came along, players did the coaching from the sidelines. Then John McGraw hired his old pal Arlie to coach for the New York Giants.

Now major league teams have as many as six coaches, some highly specialized. For instance, Willie Horton, the ex-Tiger, was Billy Martin's tranquility coach on the New York Yankees.

The coach is an important figure on a team. He is often sought out by the players as a father-confessor—a man they can tell their troubles to when they don't want to confront the fiery manager.

The coach can also soothe the feelings of the manager toward certain players. He can advise his manager about player relations. And, of course, during a game he can help with managerial strategy.

Nobody works any harder than the big league coach… and nobody is paid less. It doesn't seem right, somehow. But it's been that way since Arlie Latham, and that's probably the way it's going to stay.

★ ★ ★

Where would baseball be without the boxscore? It's the perfect condensation of a game. Nowhere in any other sport can we get such a succinct summary.

The man who gave us this little gem of the diamond was Henry Chadwick. Chadwick came up with the idea of the boxscore in 1859. As the baseball editor of the *New York Clipper*, he was covering a game in South Brooklyn between the Stars and the Excelsiors when he made his contribution to baseball recordkeeping. He adapted the boxscore from the scorecard he used in cricket, and he included the names of the players and details of their performances.

The boxscore has lasted all through the years. Sure, there have been changes, but its basic form has remained. It is must reading every day for millions of fans all over the world.

The boxscore was only one of Chadwick's gifts to baseball. In 1858 he wrote the first rule book. Fifteen years later he started the first baseball weekly, *The Ball Player's Chronicle*. In the 1870s, Chadwick led a successful crusade to rid baseball of gambling. In the 1880s he published the first fan paper of the game—*The Metropolitan*, a journal of the polo grounders. He became editor of the *Spalding Baseball Guide* in 1888 and held that job until his death in 1908.

Chadwick was awarded the Medal of Achievement at the World's Fair in 1904 and in 1938 was named by a special committee to the Baseball Hall of Fame.

Chadwick was born in England in 1824. He came to America when he was 13 years old. His first writing job was covering cricket for the *Long Island Star*. It was at a cricket game in 1856 that he observed some boys playing baseball at the edge of the cricket field. This new game enthralled him and he decided that baseball was the sport he wanted to cover. Chadwick became a one-man press association, writing for several New York papers and other eastern dailies. He began elaborate recordkeeping and became the game's first statistician. He covered baseball the rest of his life, and died at the age of 84.

His career reached into modern baseball, but it had its beginning with the very first club in baseball history, the Knickerbockers. After Chadwick's death, a large monument was erected in tribute to him in Brooklyn's Greenwood Cemetery. The monument is still there, topped with a marble baseball and surrounded by four bases.

Chadwick was called the "Father of Baseball." He gave the game many lasting gifts—and the greatest of these was the boxscore.

★ ★ ★

A young lady and I were talking about how to score a baseball game. She showed me her scorecard. From the way she had used the usual scoring symbols on the card, it was obvious that she was a real fan and that she knew how to score.

However, I was puzzled by one symbol.

"You keep score like an expert," I told her. "But what does HDWH mean?"

"Oh, that," she smiled. "That means He Deliberately Walked Him."

You wouldn't find HDWH on the scorecard of a veteran baseball writer or announcer; but it is expressive. And the lady's use of HDWH points up the fact that one way of scoring baseball is as good as the next. You can make scoring simple, or you can make it complicated.

In fact, scoring is much like baseball itself. A neophyte can understand baseball if he knows only that the team scoring the greater number of runs is the winner. Yet, a confirmed fanatic can take the game to an involved conclusion with hit-and-run signals, platooning, and other nuances of inside baseball.

The only test of a good scorer is this: Can you look at your scorecard five minutes later—or five years later—and recapitulate what happened? If you can do that with accuracy, you're a good scorer—no matter what system you use. The simplest way to score is to write in the lineup for each team and mark next to each batter's name an X or an O. X means the batter reached base; O means he didn't. However, few fans are satisfied with such a crude system. Although there is no official method, almost every scorer uses a numbering system for each defensive position—as follows:

1   for Pitcher
2   for Catcher
3   for First Baseman
4   for Second Baseman
5   for Third Baseman
6   for Shortstop
7   for Left Fielder
8   for Center Fielder
9   for Right Fielder

"Why 5 for the third baseman and 6 for the shortstop? Shouldn't it be the other way, going from first toward third?"

Those questions are thrown at all scorers. The answer goes back many years. When scoring was first devised by Henry Chadwick, the shortstop was a stepchild of the infield. So, he was numbered last.

After assigning numbers to positions, your next step is to make use of the basic symbols—such as HDWH. Some of these symbols are: E for error, K for strikeout, FC for fielder's choice, SB for stolen base, and W for walk.

If a batter makes an out, write down the number corresponding to the defensive player who handled the play. Do this in the inning the batter came to the plate. If he flied to right, write in a 9. If he grounded out, short to first, enter the play 63, or 6-3.

When I was broadcasting the Brooklyn Dodger games in 1948—my first season in the majors—television was just starting. The Brooklyn club had a TV announcer who knew little about baseball and even less about scoring. One of the veteran reporters took a look at this announcer's scorebook one afternoon and was amazed to find 3944 written next to Jackie Robinson's name.

"What does 3944 mean?" the reporter asked.

"Oh, that's easy," answered the telecaster. "39 is the Cub shortstop's uniform number, and the number on the back of the first baseman's uniform is 44. Robinson grounded out, shortstop to first base."

Well, this was against the established system, but you can't deny that the telecaster himself knew what he meant.

If you've done much scoring, you've noticed a difference in the printed scorecards. There are two basic types. Each has the lineup spaces on the left side of the page. The more popular type card has nine plain squares after each player's name and position. Another type—the kind I use—has squares, but each square has a diamond in the middle. The diamond thus divides the square into four segments.

In my system of scoring, each of the four outside segments represents a base, and I make use of the segments in moving the runners around the bases. For instance, take at look at the accompanying scorecard. It is the scoring of the 1951 Giant-Dodger playoff final which I telecast. Now, check the Giants' second inning. Irvin led off, grounding out short to first (63 in lower right-hand portion). Lockman singled as indicated by a slanted line. Bob Thomson followed with a single to left (indicated by a line slanted up to the left). Lockman moved to second on the Thomson single, so I put a 5 in the in the upper right-hand quarter (or second base quarter) of the Lockman square. I use the figure 5 because it designates Thomson's position on defense, third base.

Now, look at the Giants' seventh inning. Here you see how I indicate a run scoring. Irvin led off with a double, indicated by a straight line with a line through it. A triple would have two lines across, a home run would have three. The double is placed in the second base quarter of Irvin's square. In his third base segment, you see a 3. This means he reached third on the action of Lockman, the Giant first baseman. Next, a 5 in the lower left-hand quarter tells that he scored on the action of 5. Or, he came home when Bob Thomson flied to center field.

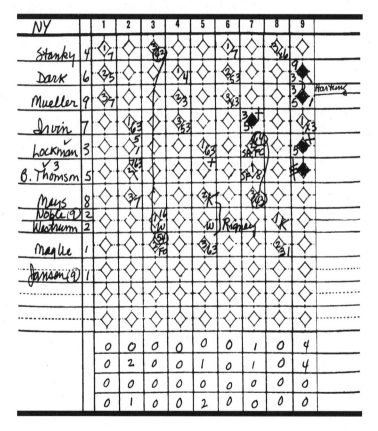

You'll notice, too, that the diamond is filled in. This is my indication for a run scored. The diamond in the box always tells what eventually happened to each batter. There are only three things which can happen:

First, he can be out. This is indicated by the number 1, 2, or 3, depending on whether the batter is the first, second, or third out of the inning.

Second, he can score. If he scores, the diamond is filled in—as in the case of Irvin.

Third, he can be left on base. In this case, an X is put into the diamond.

All the doings within the diamond give me a quick idea of what happened when I glance at my scorecard.

I embellish scoring with a few other tricks to help me in a hurry. To indicate a pop-up, I circle the number of the player who caught it. If it's foul, I put an X in front of the number. For a double play, I circle both parts of the play and join the two circles with a line. You'll see this in the seventh inning. Lockman was out at second, 64, then the batter Mays was doubled at first, 43.

When a pitching change occurs, I draw a line into the square of the first batter he'll face. Then I swing the line above the card and write in the name of the pitcher. You'll see Branca's name entered that way in the ninth inning.

I indicate RBIs by checks above the players' names in the batting order. If there are two or more RBIs, I write that number above his name. Look above Bobby Thomson's name in the lineup and you will see a check and a 3. The 3, of course, represents his famous "shot heard 'round the world." Also, I use a red pencil for all hits and runs.

This is my way. Your way is probably different. More than likely it's better. I know it's better if it tells your story of scoring the way you want it told.

The Players

4

Up For a Cup of Coffee

"Baseball gives you every chance to be great. Then it puts every pressure on you to prove that you haven't got what it takes. It never takes away the chance, and it never eases up on the pressure."—Joe Garagiola

There have probably been a lot of guys nicknamed Bobo or Bo in baseball, but the three I find most intriguing were all pitchers. Bobo Newsom, Bo Belinsky, and Bobo Holloman were all eccentric, and all three pitched no-hit games.

My old broadcasting partner and one-time Tiger manager Bob Scheffing used to talk about Holloman, the lesser-known of the trio. Bob was with the Cubs when Holloman was in spring training with that team.

Holloman had been brought up by the Cubs from Nashville. He came in with several other rookies, reporting to manager Frankie Frisch. Frisch had a terrible temper and by the fourth or fifth day of camp he had already exploded a few times.

One afternoon, after a tough exhibition loss, the Cubs filed into the clubhouse. Holloman, the rookie, yelled at his manager, Frankie Frisch: "Hey, Frank, I need a clean uniform."

Everybody looked for steam to come out of Frisch's ears. Instead, he turned and told Bobo to call the clubhouse boy. Bobo shrugged his shoulders and said to Frisch, "Frank, I thought you were the top man around here."

Scheffing asked Holloman why he did such a thing— why he took such a chance. Holloman's answer was this: "Frank didn't know me from any of the other guys, and I figured that I'd make him remember me."

Frisch did remember him...the next day he released Holloman to Shreveport.

After a couple of years in the minors, Holloman had another chance. The St. Louis Browns bought him from Syracuse just prior to the 1953 season. Holloman heard the news while he was pitching winter ball in Puerto Rico. He called Brownie owner Bill Veeck collect from the Caribbean.

"Bill," he said, "this is your new pitcher, Bobo Holloman. Congratulations on buying me. Get three more as good as me and we'll win it all."

The Browns weren't about to win anything, and the way things started in 1953, neither was Holloman. In spring training, he was hit harder than even the batting-practice pitchers. Once the season began, manager Marty Marion brought Bobo into a few games in relief. Each time he was bombed.

Veeck was ready to send his rookie pitcher back to Syracuse and recoup some of the purchase price. Going into May, Holloman's ERA was 9.0. He knew his job was on the line. He began to badger Marion to start him. Marty picked him to start, but the game was rained out. He lost another turn because of rain, but he kept after the manager to start him. Finally, on the night of May 6, 1953, Bobo Holloman, at the age of 28, made his first major league start. Fewer than 2,500 fans were in the stands in St. Louis.

Bobo Holloman proceeded to throw a no-hitter against

the Philadelphia Athletics—the only complete game in his major league career. He was the first pitcher in modern history to throw a no-hitter in his first starting assignment. Yet, within two months Holloman was back in the minors. He had only that one moment of glory.

★ ★ ★

In 1905 big league baseball was much more informal than it is now. And only in such an informal atmosphere could such a strange debut occur as that of a catcher named Gerald Shea. In those days, the St. Louis Cards had two catchers, Mike Grady and Jack Warner. And one afternoon in St. Louis, both of those catchers were injured.

A semi-pro named Gerald Shea was called from the stands to take over. He caught that afternoon and also another game for the Cards. But that was it...never again did Gerald Shea appear in a major league game. He batted .333 in those two games in 1905 and then faded from the big league scene.

Both the regular catchers had their injuries heal and were able to resume action. Where Mr. Shea went, nobody seems to know. But we do know that he had one of the quickest and one of the shortest careers in baseball . . . from right out of the grandstand and into the big leagues and then right out again.

★ ★ ★

It might be a little hard to believe this, but there was once a pitcher who won 21 games in his first and only major league season, and then decided he didn't want to pitch in the big leagues anymore. His name was Henry Schmidt.

Henry was a native of Brownsville, Texas, and was discovered by the Brooklyn Dodger manager, Ned Hanlon, while Henry was pitching at the age of 29 in the Pacific

Coast League. He came to Brooklyn and pitched for the Dodgers in 1903. He worked in 40 games. He won 21 and lost 13. Such a record these days would assure a young man of a lot of money and a very bright future, but it didn't for Henry Schmidt in 1903. Henry decided he didn't want to live—even in the summer—in the East. He would not sign a contract with Brooklyn for the 1904 baseball season and never again did he pitch another game in the majors. The 21-game winner turned in that one great year and called it quits.

★　★　★

Here's a story of a man who had a short career in base-ball, but he stuck around several seasons with the old New York Giants simply because he was a good luck charm.

The man's name was Faust, Charles Victor "Victory" Faust. One of the books says he was tall and lanky; another says he was a midget. Maybe he was somewhere in be-tween. Anyway, he presented himself to the manager of the Giants, John McGraw, during the 1911 season. While the team was taking batting practice, Faust told McGraw that a fortuneteller had told him that if he pitched for the Giants, they would win the pennant.

McGraw had heard some ridiculous stories in his hard-bitten lifetime, but this was a topper. It sounded even crazier after McGraw watched the would-be pitcher work out: Mr. Faust was no good. But, for some strange reason, McGraw took him in as mascot. The only possible explanation is that, like many old-time baseball men, McGraw was super super-stitious. Or as the man once said, "I'm not superstitious, I just don't want anything unlucky to happen to me."

Anyway, for the rest of the season, home or away, Faust would warm up in his Giant uniform before each game and then take a seat in the dugout. His teammates took a liking to him and began to make him the butt of their many pranks. They would load Faust's suitcases with bricks...they sent him out for a can of striped paint...and for the key to the pitcher's box. But he stuck around because he was a good luck charm, for during that first season of Charles Victor Faust, the Giants won the pennant. And toward the end of the year, when the pennant was clinched, McGraw put him into two games. He's in the record book: two appearances, no wins and no losses.

The next season, 1912, Faust was back again, warming up every day on the sidelines. And again the Giants won the pennant. In 1913 he was with the team again. By now, he was famous in an off-beat kind of way, and he signed for a vaudeville tour. He left the team for four games, and the Giants lost all four. So, Faust came back and the Giants again went on to win the title.

But Faust didn't last much longer. He never returned for the season of 1914. Sadly, he took up residence in a mental institution. And in 1914, the Giants did not win the pennant.

★ ★ ★

Deep in the baseball record books, you'll find the name of Jim Bluejacket. Bluejacket pitched three games for Cincinnati during the 1916 season, but his only bid to escape complete obscurity lies in his name: Bluejacket. Where would a name like that come from?

Well, Bluejacket's real name was James Smith. After he was discharged from the Navy in 1908, he reported to the Bartlesville, Oklahoma, team wearing the only clothing he had—his Navy uniform. The team had no uniform for him so he wore his Navy duds while he pitched his first game.

The local sportswriter was downright lazy, and he wasn't even interested enough to check the name of this new pitcher. He listed him in the boxscore and game story simply as Bluejacket.

Mr. Smith happened to like that name better than his

own and thus was known as Jim Bluejacket throughout his baseball career.

A lot of people will say the most astute baseball man ever was player-manager-executive Branch Rickey. Well, Rickey once said that running speed is the one talent that a player can use both on offense and defense. When Branch ran tryout camps in the 1930s for his St. Louis Cardinals, his first move was to stage a foot race among his candidates. Only the fastest-of-foot remained in camp.

Now, all of this leads up to the fact that running speed is great—but it's not everything. Remember Charlie Finley? He hired the speedster Herb Washington to "play" for his Oakland A's in 1974. Herb was with Finley for two years. He appeared in a total of 104 games and never had a time at bat. The only other figures on his stat chart were 33 runs scored and 30 stolen bases. And, if memory serves, Herb was used as a pinch-runner in the 1974 World Series and was picked off base.

The Tigers once had a man who was hired mostly for his speed, and he, too, suffered a baseball running gaff in a World Series. This was wartime baseball and the man was Chuck Hostetler. Chuck was 40 years old when he signed with the Tigers in 1944. He came out of the semi-pro ranks. Jack Zeller, Detroit general manager, had been tipped off that Hostetler could still run fast and that his speed might help the Tigers.

In his minor league days, Hostetler had been considered the fastest man in baseball. When he played for Topeka, Kansas, they called him the Topeka Tornado. Several efforts had been made for Chuck to race some of the speedsters in the big leagues, but those contests somehow never came off.

In that first wartime season, Hostetler started well . . . he was soon hitting over .400. Reality began to set in and his average dropped. But, he compiled a respectable .298 average for the season.

By World Series time the next year, Hostetler had become a part-time player—batting .159 in only 42 games and used mostly as a pinch-runner.

In the sixth game of the Series, Tiger manager Steve O'Neill used Hostetler as a pinch-hitter for Skeeter Webb. He opened the seventh inning and was safe on an error by the Cubs' Stan Hack. Hostetler moved to second on an infield out. Up stepped Doc Cramer. Cramer smashed a line drive to left, and Hostetler was off and running. Manager O'Neill, coaching at third, tried to flag down Hostetler as he charged into the base. Hostetler ignored the signal. He rounded third and headed for home, slipped, took a tumble, and Roy Hughes tagged him out. The play cost the Tigers a run and eventually a victory.

Manager O'Neill berated his speedy baserunner: "I put up my hands," said Steve, "but he paid no attention. That cost us a run and the game." Harsh words from the usually mild O'Neill.

Hostetler, hired for his speed and his baserunning ability, had those talents turn on him in the World Series—the climax of his short career. He never played again in the majors.

★ ★ ★

In 1933, a super minor league slugger named Joe Hutcheson became a member of the Brooklyn Dodgers. Joe had burned up the Southern League with his bat, and Dodger manager Max Carey had high hopes for him.

He was a great hitter all right—but only in batting practice. Against those easy tosses he would slam the ball to all corners of the park. But when the game started, it was different. The big, lumbering rookie was an easy out.

He went to bat 67 times in one stretch and all he could do was hit two weak singles. After going 0-for-7 in a doubleheader one afternoon, Big Joe came stomping into the Dodger clubhouse and roared to Carey, "The pitchers in this league don't want me to hit."

Carey slowly stroked his chin and gave Hutcheson a long and steady stare. Then Max said very softly, "You've got the idea exactly, Joe."

★ ★ ★

Cletus Elwood "Boots" Poffenberger didn't last too long in the majors. He liked his beer and his trips home to Williamsport, Maryland, too much. But he did stay around long enough to have one of the much-repeated classics of baseball pinned on him. It was Boots who one morning called room service at the hotel and asked for the "breakfast of champions."

"What's that?" asked the lady on the phone.

"You know, the breakfast of champions," repeated Boots. "A steak sandwich and six beers."

Boots says it never happened, and I'd have to believe him.

The Detroit Tigers bought Boots in 1937. Schoolboy Rowe had a sore arm, and Detroit sent Rowe to the Texas League and brought up Boots to replace him. Poffenberger was 9-1 in Texas, and with the Tigers that year he won 10 and lost 5.

The next year he missed a midnight curfew in Philadelphia. Next day, manager Mickey Cochrane approached him in the clubhouse. "Poffenberger, what time did you get in last night?"

Slowly Boots got to his feet and looked his manager right in the eye. "I refuse to reveal my identity," he said. He was fined $100 and ordered to return to Detroit. Instead, Boots headed home to Williamsport.

He returned to the club, but five weeks later was in trouble again. This time, in Washington, Cochrane told him to return to Detroit and wait for the team. Again he went instead to Williamsport. Two weeks later Boots was farmed to Toledo and finished out the season there.

Next spring when Poffenberger was 10 days late coming to Tiger spring training, the club had had enough. They sold him to Brooklyn for $25,000. Brooklyn's Leo Durocher couldn't handle Boots any better than his Tiger managers, Cochrane and Del Baker. Poffenberger lasted less than a season with the Dodgers and drifted back to the minors.

★ ★ ★

Did the great Ty Cobb have serious intentions of quitting baseball after his first few games in the majors? If he did think of quitting, how much influence was exerted on him by a letter from his manager, William Armour?

Cobb had joined the Detroit Tigers in late 1905. He played 41 games and batted only .240, showing little promise of his potential greatness.

However, what little promise he showed was recognized by Manager Armour.

Here is an excerpt from a letter which Armour wrote Cobb on January 6, 1906. (This letter is in the Ernie Harwell Collection at the Detroit Public Library.)

". . . You will find enclosed your contract made for $1,500, which is $300 more than I talked to you of before leaving. . . . Think you would be very foolish to pull away from the game at present as you have a bright future in front of you, if I am any judge of a player."

★ ★ ★

He had played baseball at Cooley High School in Detroit and also while he served in the U.S. Marines. He signed a minor league contract with the Tigers in 1952 for $3,000. He played in the Tiger system as an infielder and one season batted .340.

However, a knee injury stopped his march to the big leagues, ending his career.

So he started a successful pizza business and became an outstanding entrepreneur and civic leader.

And in 1992, 40 years later, he finally made it to the major leagues. He became the owner of the Detroit Tigers, the team he once dreamed of playing for.

So the dream did come true for Mike Ilitch, and it continues as he works to build a pennant winner for Detroit.

5

Standing the Test of Time

*"It isn't hard to be good from time to time in sports.
What's tough is being good every day."*—Willie Mays

In 1993, Nolan Ryan pitched his 27th year in the majors—
an all-time record. Right behind Ryan, and tied with
Tommy John, is James T. "Deacon" McGuire.

The Deacon is quite a story. He was born in 1863 and
grew up in Albion, Michigan. His labor there as an iron
worker built him a body that lasted longer in the big leagues
than any other position player. McGuire is buried in River-
side Cemetery in Albion, and above his tombstone two slen-
der bats are crossed—a final tribute to the man who worked
in iron and became one of baseball's true iron men.

McGuire started his big league career with Toledo of
the American Association, then a big league. He played for
12 different teams. And he played for Detroit in two different leagues—the National in the 1880s and the American
League in the 1900s.

The Deacon was a catcher: He had 10 broken fingers to
prove it. McGuire's early reputation as a hitter and a good

catcher was established when he played for a town team in Hastings, Michigan. He was the only youngster who could handle the famous snake ball of Charles "Lady" Baldwin, who later pitched for the National League Detroit team and is buried in Hastings.

McGuire's first year at Toledo saw him catch another famous big leaguer, Tony "The Count" Mullane, who threw with either arm. He was also a teammate of Moses Fleetwood Walker, the first black player in major league history.

The Deacon, during his 26 big league seasons, was a manager three different times. His first year of managing was with Washington in 1898, but later in the 1990s he managed both Boston and Cleveland.

McGuire's final full year as a player came in 1910 with Cleveland. But in 1912 he became a scout for the Tigers, and that was the affiliation that returned him to the playing ranks one more time.

The Tigers went on strike in 1912 after Ty Cobb fought a fan in New York and was suspended by American League president Ban Johnson. The Tigers refused to play a game in Philadelphia against the Athletics. A forfeit was bad enough, but if no players showed up, the Detroit club would be assessed a fine of $5,000. Manager Hughey Jennings had to search for replacements. He combed the sandlots and the college ranks until he came up with some bodies. He added McGuire to that lineup and the old Deacon was back in action—at the age of 48. The Tigers lost that day, 24-2. McGuire had a walk, scored a run, and made three errors. But his 26th season got him in the recordbook.

The Deacon continued to scout for the Tigers until 1924. In 1926 he coached baseball at Albion and later retired to his farm just outside that town.

★ ★ ★

There are big league stars who make a lot of noise and get a lot of headlines. There are others who are quiet, do the job with real efficiency, and hardly ever get noticed by anybody. The Tigers had one of the quiet and efficient types in the 1940s. His name was Roger Cramer, but everybody called him Doc. He spent 20 years in the American League —the last seven in Detroit. He broke in with the Philadelphia Athletics and also played for the Boston Red Sox and the Washington Senators.

The headlines didn't come to Doc, probably because he was not a home run hitter: He hit only 37 roundtrippers in his lifetime. In his five years with the Red Sox, he hit only one ball out of Fenway Park. But he compiled some good figures: a .296 lifetime batting average, 2,705 hits, and his putouts-per-game ratio was higher than that of Willie Mays.

Cramer got into the pros because in Pennsylvania in 1929 it was still unlawful to play baseball on Sunday. So, Cy Perkins and Jimmy Dykes of the Philadelphia A's happened to be in Cramer's hometown of Beach Haven, New Jersey, one Sunday, and they saw Doc pitching for the semipro team there. They invited him to Shibe Park for a workout, and he was signed by Connie Mack.

Mack sent Cramer to Martinsburg, West Virginia, with instructions to the manager, Dan O'Leary, to make Cramer into a center fielder. He became one of the best.

Cramer did pitch one time in the majors. It happened in Boston in 1938. The Red Sox were losing by a lopsided score, and manager Joe Cronin called him in from the outfield to pitch. He worked four innings, allowed a couple of runs, and three hits. But he didn't give up his day job as a center fielder.

When Cramer was traded to the Tigers in December 1941, most baseball people felt he didn't have many years left. He fooled 'em. He played until he was 43 years old and stayed with the Tigers for seven good years. The deal that sent Doc to Detroit involved three other players. The Tigers got Cramer and infielder Jimmy Bloodworth and gave up Bruce Campbell and Frank Croucher. Bloodworth had one of the toughest jobs in the history of the Tigers: He had to replace Charlie Gehringer at second base.

Cramer's best Tiger season was 1943. He hit an even .300 and stroked 182 hits. He turned in an outstanding performance in the 1945 World Series when the Tigers beat the Cubs. Doc had 11 hits in the Series and batted .379.

Cramer played his last game as a Tiger in 1948, completing 20 years in the big leagues as a fine, steady performer. The last I heard of Doc, he was living in Manhawkin, New Jersey, just a few miles from where Jimmy Dykes and Cy Perkins discovered him on that Sunday afternoon back in 1929.

★ ★ ★

He was not a great ballplayer, but he was my kind of guy. Dick McAuliffe, the Tiger infielder of the 1960s, was a blue-collar kind of player in a blue-collar town.

The '68 season epitomized his career. His stats weren't great in that best season of his, but he was steady. He batted .249 and had 16 home runs with his patented wide-open stance, and managed to lead the league in runs scored with 95. And when he was suspended for five days in mid-season, the Tigers went into a spin. They recovered and went on to win the pennant, but for those five days they sure missed Dick McAuliffe.

The Tigers were playing the White Sox that night at Tiger Stadium, August 22. Dick charged the mound after Tommy John had fired three pitches over his head. They fought and John injured his shoulder. American League president Joe Cronin fined Dick $500 and suspended him for five days. While he was out, the Detroiters won only one game, lost five, and their seven-and-a-half-game lead dropped to five.

Mac had been a shortstop most of his career but made a switch to second base during 1967 when Ray Oyler took over shortstop. Dick was the American League shortstop in the All-Star Games of 1965 and '67. It was Tiger manager Mayo Smith who switched him to second, and he adjusted there easily. It even seemed to be a better position for him.

In high school Dick had been a pitcher. Scout Lou Cassell was watching him pitch one day when the first 11 pitches he threw in a game were out of the strike zone. The coach came out and switched McAuliffe to third base. Anyway, Lou signed him, and Dick got a bonus of $380. He started at Erie, Pennsylvania, in 1957 and climbed his way to the top. He was with the Tigers from 1960 through the 1973 season.

McAuliffe always said that Frank Skaff did the most for his career. In 1959, Dick was sent from Knoxville to Durham, where Skaff was the manager. Dick had trouble with his temper at Knoxville, but Frankie calmed him down, worked hard with him, and made him a better player.

You'll remember that later Skaff became a Tiger manager for a few weeks during the '66 season. By then McAuliffe was a regular big leaguer.

Dick's proudest moment in his career came in the 1965 All-Star Game at Minnesota. He hit a home run to deep center field off Jim Maloney of the Cincinnati Reds.

But most of the time McAuliffe was just a steady, plodding type of player. In 16 seasons, he hit .247 with 197 homers and 697 RBIs. He was a popular, gutsy, little guy who played hard and loved to win.

★ ★ ★

Still regarded as the premier center fielder by all the old-timers, Tris Speaker had a great career. He broke in back in 1907 and lasted until 1928. He was on championship teams in both Boston and Cleveland, and was the

manager of the Indians when they took the American
League pennant in 1920. In 22 years in the majors he compiled a lifetime batting average of .344.

Speaker was left in Little Rock by the Red Sox in 1908 in
payment for the rent of the ballpark during spring training.
But later that year, when he was burning up the minors,
Boston bought him back, and he stayed for the next 21
years in the majors with the Red Sox, Cleveland, Washington, and Philadelphia.

Tris' greatest fame came from his fielding. He has been
regarded as the best in going back on a fly. He played very
shallow in center field, so close that he sometimes would
pounce on a grounder and throw the batter out at first base.

Twice in one month Speaker pulled unassisted double
plays—the same way. With a man on second and none out,
the batter hit a screaming line drive over second base. Since
it looked like a single, the runner on second took off right
away. Speaker charged in from his shallow center field,
grabbed the ball on the run, and touched second before the
embarrassed runner could get back to the bag.

Speaker was a handsome man, with a ruddy complex-
ion and gray hair. Throughout most of his career he bore
the nickname, "The Grey Eagle."

Some of the more recent baseball observers vouch for
Joe DiMaggio as the greatest of center fielders, but the old-
timers all cast their ballots for Tris Speaker. Truly, Tris was
deserving of his early election to the Baseball Hall of Fame,
and he's certain to be mentioned any time the talk comes
around to great outfielding.

★ ★ ★

Detroit will remember Harvey Kuenn as a Rookie-of-
the-Year shortstop for the 1953 Tigers and the 1959 American League batting champion.

In Milwaukee, Harvey made baseball history when he

became interim manager of the Brewers in June 1982 and led his team to its only American League pennant.

Kuenn was a hard-nosed player and a no-nonsense manager. His teammates respected him, and the athletes who played for him had a true devotion to him.

That championship Brewers team was the pride of Kuenn's career. It slammed 216 home runs and had the nickname of "Harvey's Wallbangers." Kuenn was named Manager of the Year by the Associated Press and United Press International.

Kuenn also had a personal triumph over physical hardships. The word "courage" truly fit him. Harvey suffered a heart attack in 1976. He also had major stomach surgery, and his right leg was amputated below the knee. Through it all, he kept his spirit and sense of humor. He never asked for pity or special favors.

Kuenn, born in West Allis, Wisconsin, excelled in basketball and baseball at the University of Wisconsin. He signed a bonus contract with the Tigers in 1952, spending his only minor league season at Davenport.

In Kuenn's first full season, 1953, he was named Rookie of the Year by *The Sporting News* and the Baseball Writers Association of America. He led the league in hits (209) and at-bats (679), and still holds American League rookie records for at-bats and singles (167).

Tigers Hall-of-Famer Al Kaline has fond memories of his early years with Kuenn.

"When I joined the Tigers," Al recalls, "Harvey looked after me. We were both young, and he made me feel that I was part of the team.

"It seemed that he could hit a line drive almost anytime he wanted. He never cared who was pitching; he knew he could hit. He was one of the best strike-two hitters I ever saw."

Kuenn spent eight years with the Tigers and made the All-Star team eight times (there were two games in 1959).

He batted more than .300 his first four full seasons. His .353 average won the American League batting title in 1959.

At the close of spring training in 1960, Kuenn was traded by the Tigers to Cleveland for Rocky Colavito. It was a blockbuster deal—Kuenn, the batting champion, for Colavito, who with 42 had shared the American League home run title the previous season with Harmon Killebrew.

From Cleveland, Kuenn went on to play for the San Francisco Giants and the Chicago Cubs. He finished his career in 1966 with the Philadelphia Phillies.

I can still picture Kuenn, leaning into a fastball and slapping a hard line drive to right.

★ ★ ★

The greatest team he ever played for brought Harry Loran "Nemo" Leibold his greatest heartbreak. At the height of his major league career he was an outfielder for the scandal-ridden Chicago White Sox of 1919.

"What a great team!" exclaimed Leibold. "It was a reeling blow to us when investigations in September 1920 proved the 1919 Series had been fixed. We could not believe that eight of our teammates let us down."

The Sox should also have won the 1920 pennant, according to Leibold. They were in the thick of the race when the scandal broke. With the team split by dissension and the nucleus of the club suspended, the Sox lost the flag to Cleveland.

Nemo's roommate was George "Buck" Weaver, third baseman and one of the eight tainted White Sox. "I roomed with Buck throughout the 1919 and 1920 seasons, and never had an inkling there was anything wrong," said Leibold.

Leibold tagged Weaver as the greatest of all third basemen. "He used to have trouble hitting the curve right-handed," said Nemo. "Know what he did? Taught himself to bat left-handed. Then, in mid-season he became a switch-hitter for the rest of his career."

When Leibold played for Chicago he shared the right-field spot with John "Shano" Collins. Joe Jackson and Oscar Felsch, the other two outfielders, played regularly. "I get a laugh," said Nemo, "when some of the new fans tell me that platooning is a recent development. It was going a long time before I came along."

Nemo was only 5-feet-5$\frac{1}{2}$ inches tall and weighed just 150 pounds during his playing career. He starred in the American League for 13 years with Cleveland, Chicago, Boston, and Washington. He played in four World Series: 1917 and 1919 with the White Sox, and 1924 and 1925 with the Senators.

Did he ever regret being so small?

"No," he answers. "As a matter of fact, it might have been an advantage. I was leadoff man and was hard to pitch to. Also, I had speed and could hit to any field. In those days of the dead ball, lack of height didn't seem to be harmful."

It was Jimmy Barrett, one-time Tiger outfielder, who brought Leibold into baseball. Jimmy came home to Detroit after managing the Oshkosh, Wisconsin, team in 1910. He saw Nemo on the sandlots, liked him, and signed Nemo and three other Detroiters. When Barrett switched to Milwaukee, he took Leibold there for his pro debut in 1911. Two years later Nemo was in the big leagues—at Cleveland. There he picked up his nickname. Jack Lelivelt, the Cleveland outfielder, called him "Little Nemo," after a popular comic strip character.

In 1915 Nemo was traded to Chicago and stayed there until the spring of 1921. Then he went to the Red Sox and ended his career with Washington in 1924 and 1925.

One of the highlights of his career came in the seventh game of the 1924 World Series. Leibold led off the eighth inning with a pinch-hit double to start a two-run rally. The rally tied the game and the Senators finally won with a run in the 12th to take the championship.

In the late '20s Leibold became a manager at Columbus, Ohio. He played until 1931 and then continued to manage. He finished his career as pilot of the Toledo team in 1949.

★ ★ ★

One of the steadiest ballplayers I've seen was Eddie Brinkman. "Steady" Eddie was an outstanding shortstop for the Tigers in 1971-74. He didn't always get the credit he deserved playing in the shadows of Al Kaline, Willie Horton, Mickey Lolich, and Bill Freehan.

In 1972, Brinkman played 72 straight errorless games, still an American League record for shortstops. He had 331 straight errorless chances and made only seven errors in 156 games. It was no surprise that Ed won a Gold Glove. He teamed with third baseman Aurelio Rodriguez on an outstanding left side of the infield. Not many grounders eluded the two dandies.

Rodriguez and Brinkman came to the Tigers in the same trade—one of the best the Tigers ever made. Bob Short was the owner of the Washington Senators at the time, and he coveted Tigers' righthander Denny McLain. For two years, Short tried to talk general manager Jim Campbell into trading Denny. Finally, Campbell made the deal that paid big dividends for Detroit. Brinkman, Rodriguez, and pitchers Joe Coleman and Jim Hannan became Tigers; the Senators got McLain, third baseman Don Wert, lefthander Norm McRae, and outfielder Elliott Maddox.

Brinkman was an outstanding schoolboy star in Cincinnati. He was born there and attended Western Hills High. Eddie played on the same high school baseball team as Pete Rose. And Brinkman never played for a winner until 1972 when the Tigers won the American League East. Brinkman says that was the biggest thrill in his baseball career.

With the Tigers, he roomed with Frank Howard, who

was the biggest guy on the team. Eddie was one of the smallest—slightly built, but tough and wiry.

After the East-clinching win in 1972, Brinkman let slip a remark that is still part of Tiger lore. A happy and champagne-soaked Brinkman told a TV reporter, "This team is the greatest bleeping bunch of guys I've ever played with." For a long time, Eddie's teammates never let him forget that slip of the tongue.

Brinkman was traded to San Diego after the '74 season. But he never played for the Padres. They dealt him to St. Louis, where he played 28 games in 1975. He joined the Rangers and Yankees before retiring after the '75 season.

Brinkman hit .224 during a 15-year career, but he was one of the best and steadiest shortstops.

He returned to the Tigers in 1976 as an instructor in the farm system. He also managed in the Tigers' system and coached at Detroit one year.

From 1983 through 1992 he was a coach with the White Sox. Brinkman had heart bypass surgery and recovered in fine shape. He's now a superscout for the White Sox.

★ ★ ★

An outstanding shortstop historically symbolizes each of the Chicago teams. The Cubs on the north side salute Ernie Banks; the south side White Sox look to Luke Appling. Banks, retired for many years, still beams, "Let's play two." Luke died in 1991 but remains the consummate White Sox star.

Most people remember Luke as the champion at fouling off pitches until he got a good one. Some recall him as the outstanding Sick Man of Baseball.

I wrote an article about Luke for *Sport* magazine in 1948 and titled it "The Sick Man of Baseball." The whole point of the piece was that the worse Luke felt, the better he played. He was always moaning about his health. Nobody resented that because they all knew Luke didn't mean it. He would moan, but he still had that happy pixie grin that told all of us how much he enjoyed baseball and life in general. Appling was one of my boyhood heroes. He grew up in Atlanta, my hometown. My first memory of Luke goes back to 1930, when he hit four homers in one game for his Oglethorpe College team.

After college he immediately signed with the Atlanta Crackers. He hit .326 that first year, and Crackers owner Rell J. Spiller sold him to the White Sox. Strangely enough, Luke almost became a Cub. Spiller thought he had a deal with William Veeck, the Cubs' president. He even wired Luke (on a trip with the Crackers to Little Rock) that the Cubs had acquired him.

But the transaction fell through. Spiller then contacted the White Sox. Chicago sent Atlanta $20,000, plus an outfielder, Poco Taitt, to complete the transaction.

Luke lasted 20 years, all with the White Sox. In 1964 he was selected to the Hall of Fame. Later, he gained a new notoriety when, at 72, he banged a home run in the Crackerjack Old-Timers Game in Washington.

The story that best characterized Old Aches and Pains happened early in his career. Luke built a fine home on the outskirts of Atlanta. The centerpiece of the Appling estate was a lake where Luke loved to fish. When the Applings were in Chicago for the summer, the neighborhood kids often disregarded Luke's "No Fishing" sign. The caretaker wired Appling and asked: "Is it all right for the kids to fish in your lake?"

Appling wired back. "OK for kids to fish in lake. Don't let them know I said so. It might spoil their fun."

The happy moaner Luke Appling was a great friend and companion. Like Banks is to the Cubs, Luke is the symbol of the White Sox history.

★ ★ ★

Die-hard Tiger fans will remember the Detroit-Texas game when the Tigers ran out of catchers and pressed Tom Brookens into service.

Brookens called it the highlight of his baseball life—the one and only time he ever caught in a game. That was typical of Tommy. He was always ready to help—truly a team man. Never a star, he was one of the most popular players in Tigers history with teammates and fans. Many hearts were broken when the Tigers traded Brookens to the Yankees for pitcher Charles Hudson in the spring of 1989.

But back to that amazing performance on July 20, 1985, when third baseman Brookens became a catcher. Starter Lance Parrish was hurt. Sparky Anderson started Bob Melvin as his catcher. Marty Castillo replaced him and left for a pinch-hitter. During a rally, Brookens was standing on first. He looked over to first base coach Dick Tracewski.

"Trixie," Brookens said, "if we tie this game, somebody's gotta catch."

"Yeah," Tracewski answered. "And it's gonna be you."

The Tigers did tie the game. Brookens went to the dugout and looked at Sparky. Anderson nodded and Tom put on Parrish's shin guards and chest protector — Parrish at 6-foot-3, 210 pounds and Brookens only 5-foot-11 and 165. Tommy could hardly get up the dugout steps. He sort of stumbled his way toward the plate.

The Tigers' pitcher was Aurelio Lopez. Lopez called Brookie to the mound. He told him just to put down one finger for every pitch. He would throw only fast balls.

It worked. Tommy caught four innings and the Tigers won, 6-5, in the 15th.

Brookens' last season with the Tigers was 1988. In the following spring Detroit traded him to the Yankees for Hudson. He platooned at third base with Mike Pagliarulo. Then he was injured.

He became a free agent and signed with Cleveland for

1990. The Indians used him as a utility man. When the season was over, they showed no interest in Brookens.

Away from baseball now, Tommy is left with the memories of Tigers days and the many friends who appreciated his loyalty and team spirit.

He will forever remember that one game against Texas when he became a catcher for the first and last time.

★ ★ ★

Dave Bergman found out early that life wasn't always going to be easy. When he was old enough to understand, he discovered that his older brother Steve was severely retarded.

Steve is still alive, 41 years old but bedridden, blind, and unable to speak.

Through it all, Bergman came to realize how important health is. Whenever he begins to feel sorry for himself, he thinks of Steve and his struggles, and realizes how lucky he is.

Bergman, now retired after almost 20 years in baseball, ended his career as a top-notch utility man.

Dave was born in Evanston, Illinois, and grew up as an avid Cubs fan. The Cubs drafted him when he finished high school, but Dave valued a college education, bypassed pro ball, and enrolled at Illinois State. He starred there in baseball and at the end of his junior year, 1974, the Yankees drafted him in the second round.

The Yankees started Dave at Oneonta. He hit .348 and 10 home runs in 56 games and was selected the New York-Penn League's Most Valuable Player. The next season he was just as good. He was the Eastern League's batting champion with a .311 average at West Haven. He again won the MVP title.

Was he really that good? Bergman says he simply worked harder than the others, always bearing down and pushing himself.

A short trip at the end of that 1975 season to the Yankees brought Dave in touch with reality. Called up in late August, he appeared in seven games and failed to get a hit in 17 at-bats.

Bergman did some soul-searching and decided he had to work harder. For the next five years he played winter ball, two years in Venezuela and three years in Puerto Rico. After two years, the talent-laden Yankees traded Dave to Houston. It was there he learned to be a utility player — a role that kept him in the majors for 15 full seasons. He learned how to fill in where the team needed him and to master the very difficult art of pinch-hitting.

Bergman credits his success to Houston manager Bill Virdon, who was tough but very patient. He was a father, a friend, and an outstanding manager to Bergie.

During his fourth year at Houston, Dave was traded to San Francisco. His final year there, 1983, he hit .432 in August and .351 in September. He batted .351 as a pinch-hitter. Dave enjoyed playing for Frank Robinson. Frank taught him how to think on the diamond and how to do a lot of the little—but important—things.

The Giants traded Dave to the Phillies in March 1984, but the Phils immediately sent him to Detroit, along with Willie Hernandez, for Glenn Wilson and John Wockenfuss.

Tigers fans remember Bergman for a time at bat as a pinch-hitter in the pennant-winning season of 1984. With a 3-2 count, Dave fouled off 13 of Toronto's Roy Lee Jackson's pitches. Then he hit a three-run homer to beat the Blue Jays.

That time at bat typified Bergman—hard-working, talented, and tough.

★ ★ ★

Nobody knew when Leroy "Satchel" Paige was born, but everybody agreed he was born 25 years too soon.

When Paige was at his peak, organized baseball belonged solely to the white man. Instead of grabbing major league headlines and making the Hall of Fame, the lean Paige was rubber-arming his way toward a legendary stardom on the ragged diamonds of obscure villages. By the time he reached the majors, Paige was a spindly relic of his own greatness. When he left the big leagues at the age of 48 (estimated), he had been more of a box-office attraction than a winning pitcher.

As early as 1926, Satch might have pitched a game in organized ball if he hadn't lost faith in a can of whitewash. Paige was with Alex Herman's Black Lookouts in Chattanooga, and Strande Nicklin, president of the White Lookouts of the Southern Association, offered him $500 to pitch against the Atlanta Crackers.

"We'll paint you white," Nicklin told him. "They won't know the difference."

Satch was willing. But Herman convinced him it wouldn't work—the paint would wash off during the game.

However, during his career Paige was to pitch against the greatest white stars. After the 1934 World Series, Satch faced the Dean Brothers and a team of major league stars. He worked for the first six innings, striking out 16 of the 18 batters. Not a man reached first.

"If some big league club had signed Paige that year," said Ray Doan, who promoted the game, "Satch would have gone down in history as the greatest pitcher of all time."

In another game, Paige was locked in a pitching duel with Dizzy Dean. With the score nothing to nothing in the 10th, Diz came to bat.

"Mr. Dean," announced Paige, "if you ain't gonna give us no runs, we ain't gonna give you none."

Dean tripled. Satch turned toward third and said, "Mr. Dean, you'd better take a good rest—you ain't going no further."

Paige was right. He blanked Dizzy's team and won in the 13th, 1-0.

It was after that duel that Dean paid the skinny pitcher a great tribute. "Satch and me," he said, "would be worth a quarter of a million to any club. We'd clinch the pennant by July 4th and go fishing till the World Series. Between us, we'd win 60."

When somebody passed along these words to Paige, he replied, "Heck, *I'd* win 60."

One year, on his cross-country journeys, Satch won 54 games and lost only four. In his almost 30-year career Paige pitched in more than 5,000 games. How many he won is anybody's guess, but Paige himself claims he pitched a "hatful of no-hitters."

He was as good as his word, and his word for himself was "the greatest." On his big cerise auto was written "World's Greatest Pitcher." And one season he advertised a guarantee to strike out the first nine men in a game.

Paige was a man unto himself. His auto and his guitar were his companions. He trained his own way. St. Louis Browns' manager Rogers Hornsby tried to insist that Satch follow the club's strict training regimen. Satch attempted it, but could not stand the pace. He ambled up to Hornsby. "Mr. Hornsby," he asked, "are you training ol' Satch for pitching baseball or are you trying to train him for the Army?"

Paige kept in shape. His arm was never sore. Only his stomach bothered him. Quick trips to faraway playing fields, eating on the run, and sleeping in his auto took their toll: None of these professional demands was any aid to the wizard's digestion.

Bad stomach or not, Satch was a pro. He was a very fine fielding pitcher, never making an error during his five-year major league career. In his earlier days he often played outfield between pitching assignments. However, his outfielding came to an abrupt halt one afternoon in Venezuela. Paige sauntered back for a flyball and was about to step over what he thought was a piece of black rubber hose. Then it moved—like a snake. Satch moved, too. He outran the ball, the python, and the field. It was then he decided he'd stick to pitching.

He really stuck with it one season when he pitched 30 days in a row. And though his travel schedule would have scared an airline hostess, he could produce when he had to.

In 1934, Paige drove all night from Pittsburgh to New York for a game the next afternoon. He parked his auto on the streets of Harlem in the early morning and slept until just before game time. With the score tied in the 11th, Satch got careless. He walked the first three batters, then struck out the next three. His team scored in the last half of the 11th, and Satch went back to his car to sleep.

When Paige came belatedly to the majors his speed was gone, but he still had cunning. He helped pitch the Cleveland Indians to a pennant in his first year, 1948. However, his only World Series appearance lasted less than an inning in a game already lost. Satch was ready when his All-Star Game chance arrived, but rain shortened the game and cheated him out of his turn.

Those two events were symbolic of the man's career. He was great. His greatness was recognized, but he was unlucky: His skin was black, and he was born too soon.

★ ★ ★

When Satchel was in his mid-40s and pitching for the St. Louis Browns, he took very little time to warm up. Once, 15 minutes before a game, his manager Zach Taylor told him:

"Satch, it's time to warm up."

"I'll be ready," Satch told him, but made no move from the bench.

With 10 minutes to go, Satch had still not warmed up. Taylor reminded him again.

"I'll be ready," Satch told him. Still, he didn't warm up. Now manager Taylor was at the plate with the lineups. He looked over to the Browns' dugout, nodded to Satch, and the ancient pitcher ambled up the dugout steps. As Taylor completed the pre-game conference, Satch made two practice tosses and strolled out to the mound, ready to start the game.

Paige never knew who the next opposing hitter might be. Once he called Freddie Marsh, his third baseman, over to the mound.

"How 'bout this guy?" Satchel asked.

"It's Ted Williams," Marsh answered.

"No, no," said Paige. "I don't care 'bout his name. Is he gonna bat right or left-handed? That's all I want to know."

6

Trading Places

*"Being traded is like celebrating your hundredth birthday.
It might not be the happiest occasion in the world,
but consider the alternatives."*—Joe Garagiola

Trades have always been a big part of baseball, and I think
the fans usually get a kick out of hearing about them.
When I was announcing in Baltimore, the Orioles pulled off
the biggest trade in baseball history. In the fall of 1954—
after Baltimore's first year in the big leagues—the Orioles
and the Yankees made a deal that involved 17 players.

Jimmy Dykes had managed Baltimore in its first season,
and Arthur Ehlers was the general manager. But owner
Clarence Miles made a quick change and brought in Paul
Richards from the White Sox to serve in a dual role—manager and general manager. Paul got busy and made that
blockbuster deal with George Weiss, general manager of
the Yankees.

Some of those 17 players were big stars, others were only
supporting players. Probably the two biggest names —in
hindsight—were Don Larsen and Bob Turley, both Baltimore pitchers who went to the New Yorkers. Larsen pitched
the only perfect game in World Series history for the Yanks,
and Turley had some outstanding seasons in his eight-year

77

Yankee career. His best season was 1958, when he won 21 games and then added two World Series victories.

In addition to Turley and Larsen, the Yankees acquired Billy Hunter, Dick Kryhoski, Darrell Johnson, Mike Blyzka, and Jim Fridley. In return, Baltimore acquired Harry Byrd, Jim McDonald, Bill Miller, Gus Triandos, Hal Smith, Gene Woodling, Ted Del Guercio, Willie Miranda, Kal Segrist, and Don Leppert. Ten Yankees went to Baltimore and seven Orioles to the Yankees.

The newspaperman who broke the trade story was the late Joe Reichler. At that time Joe was the baseball editor for the Associated Press. He was at home one Friday night in November when he got a phone call from Frank Lane, then general manager for the White Sox. Frank told him about the 17-man deal.

Reichler asked Lane if he was drunk.

"I've never had a drink in my life," Lane told him.

Reichler sat down and wrote the story. He phoned his AP office, where Orlo Robertson was on the desk. As soon as he told him about the 17 players, Orlo said, "C'mon, Joe, are you drunk?"

Joe told him no, this was really a 17-man deal, and the story went on the wire.

★ ★ ★

Most trades come out fairly even. It's very unusual for one general manager or owner to skin another one. The proverbial trade that helps both teams is the ideal one. If it's too one-sided, the offended party might not come back for another deal. But, believe me, there have been exceptions.

Generally speaking, baseball historians point to a turn-of-the-century transaction as the most one-sided of all time. In 1900, the New York Giants acquired Christy Mathewson from the Cincinnati Reds for another right-handed pitcher, Amos Rusie. Rusie was the outstanding pitcher of his time.

He had been a big winner for years. 'Tis said that when the distance of the mound to the plate was changed in the 1890s, it was done to negate the effectiveness of Rusie's famous fastball. Mathewson was 19 years old and untried. But he went on to win 373 games in a brilliant career. Rusie developed a sore arm and never won another game.

The Reds—who lost Matty—gained a superstar via trade in 1971. This, too, was one of the most one-sided ever. Cincinnati acquired George Foster from the San Francisco Giants for Frank Duffy and Vern Geishert.

The Yankees in their long history made some great deals, among them the trade that brought Red Ruffing from the Boston Red Sox for outfielder Cedric Durst and $50,000, quite a sum in that depression year of 1930. Ruffing pitched until 1947 and went on to the Hall of Fame with a total of 273 victories. Durst was out of baseball the year after the trade.

One of the worst deals the Tigers ever made happened in 1948. The Detroiters sent a fine little lefthander named Billy Pierce and $10,000 to the Chicago White Sox in exchange for catcher Aaron Robinson. Pierce had pitched briefly for the Tigers in 1945 and '48. Detroit wanted a lefthanded-hitting catcher, and the White Sox needed pitching. Chicago asked for Art Houtteman or Ted Gray, but the Tigers didn't want to give up either of those. Instead, they sent Pierce. Billy, a Highland Park native, pitched 18 years in the majors, won more than 200 games, and pitched in two World Series.

Robinson stayed with the Tigers only two years and finished his career at Boston. Robinson's rock is still remembered as one of the outstanding boners in Detroit history. In a crucial game in 1950, Aaron failed to tag Cleveland's Bob Lemon in a play at the plate. Robinson, thinking he had a force play, tagged the plate instead, and the Tigers lost a tough one to Cleveland.

Another deal that backfired for the Tigers came at the

winter meeting in 1977 when they shipped Ben Oglivie to Milwaukee for pitcher Jim Slaton. Slaton went free agent and returned to Milwaukee after one mediocre Tiger season. Oglivie developed into a true home run hitter and RBI man for the Brewers and gave them several productive years.

On the positive side, how about Steve Demeter to the Indians for Norman Cash? That 1960 deal paid longtime dividends for Detroit. Norm hit 373 Tiger home runs and won a batting title. Demeter appeared in four games for Cleveland and never had a hit—much less a home run.

Another great Tiger deal sent Denny McLain, Don Wert, Norm McRae, and Elliott Maddox to Washington in the fall of 1970. The Tigers acquired a fine left side of the infield in Ed Brinkman and Aurelio Rodriguez, as well as a two-time 20-game winner, Joe Coleman, and another pitcher named Jim Hannan.

★ ★ ★

Trading isn't easy, and there's an adage in baseball that some of the best trades are the ones you never make. Take the case of the great Ty Cobb. In March of 1907, the Tigers proposed a trade with the Cleveland Indians. Detroit would give up the youthful Cobb for the Cleveland veteran, Elmer Flick. Flick had led the American League in hitting two years before and was an established player. Cobb was just starting his second full year with the Tigers. He had batted .320 the year before, but had been in numerous fights with his teammates and had proved a tough man to integrate into the team.

Hughie Jennings, the Tiger manager, was all for the trade. The club president, Frank Navin, didn't agree with Jennings, but was willing to go along.

On March 18, 1907, Navin wrote to Jennings: "It seems hard to think that such a mere boy as Cobb can make so much disturbance. On last year's form, he had a chance to be one of the grandest ballplayers in the country. He has everything in his favor. It would not surprise me at all to see him lead the league this year in hitting, and he has a chance to play for 15 years yet." (Cobb did lead the league that year in hitting—.350—and he played not 15 more years, but 22.)

Back to Navin's letter: "Flick is a dangerous man to bother with for the reason that he has about all the money he cares for, does not care about playing ball, except as a means of livelihood and is liable to quit on you at any time, besides being a great deal older than Cobb."

Cleveland promptly rejected the proposal in any case, since they felt Cobb's career as a troublemaker had only just begun.

In four years, Flick was gone from the majors, and Cobb stayed to be baseball's greatest player. It was the best trade the Tigers never made.

★ ★ ★

Occasions of baserunners going from first to third on a bunt, or scoring from first on a pop-fly single aren't that uncommon, but how about a player who went from first to Houston on a pop fly?

It goes back a ways…back to a man named Clarence "Heine" Mueller. Heine died in 1975, but his old managers still remember the way he ran the bases…and when they remember, they shudder.

Mueller was in the major leagues for 11 years—with the Cardinals, the Giants, the Boston Braves, and the old St. Louis Browns. Later, after his playing days were over, he served as a scout for the Cards.

He was a favorite player of Branch Rickey, and it was Rickey who gave Mueller his nickname, Heine, because of his German background.

Rickey was managing the Cards back in 1922 when

Mueller pulled one of his many boneheaded baserunning stunts. Heine singled and was perched on first base. The next batter lifted a pop foul behind the plate. The catcher made an easy catch of the fly, but Heine, for some unknown reason, was running. Head down, he kept chugging around the bases and wound up at third base. Naturally, he was doubled-off first with ease.

That night Mueller was released to Houston, a Cardinal farm club. He put it this way: "I'm the only player who went from first to Houston on a pop foul."

★ ★ ★

Does a minor leaguer ever turn down the chance to make the majors?

Former manager Ralph Houk says that in his 20-year managing career he saw it happen twice—both times when he was directing the Denver club in the New York Yankee farm system.

"I got a phone call one morning," Houk remembers. "The Yankees wanted to bring up Don Larsen, who was having a great season for us in Denver. I tried to find Larsen and couldn't locate him. I finally found him in a movie theater."

He was sitting there, eating popcorn and watching the movie.

"Hey, Don," Houk told him. "Good news. You've been recalled by the Yankees. They want you to report right away."

"But, Skipper, I don't want to go."

"Don't want to go?" Houk couldn't believe it.

"That's right," Don answered. "I like it here. I'm having a good year. Having fun, too. This is a great bunch of guys. I don't want to leave."

Houk led Larsen out of the theater. He talked to Don for another 30 minutes and convinced him to go to New York.

Larsen reported to the Yanks and eventually contributed one of the most outstanding performances in World Series history—his perfect game against the Dodgers in 1956.

Houk's other recalcitrant minor leaguer didn't belong to the Yankees. He was Carlos Paula, on loan to Denver from the Washington Senators. The Senators informed Houk they were recalling Paula. But the player didn't want to go. No special reason. He just liked Denver and was hitting well.

Again, Houk had an argument on his hands. This time it took longer; but he finally convinced Paula to report.

Paula reluctantly left Denver and joined the Washington club in Chicago—10 days late. Where he kept himself all that time between Denver and Chicago, nobody knows.

People in the baseball business simply assume that every player dreams of being a big leaguer and just can't wait to get to the majors. Yet, as Ralph Houk discovered early in his managing career at Denver, some of them don't really care that much.

★ ★ ★

Under the sun's hot glare down south each spring, major league ballplayers begin the painful routine of shedding winter fat and limbering up stiffened muscles. Throughout the spring training grind they'll be lashed on by baseball's ever-present threat: Look sharp or be traded. For most of them, the buyer would have to shell out thousands of dollars or other ballplayers. In baseball's poorer days, however, players were traded for whatever a hard-pressed club owner might need—and he could need almost anything.

Take Joe Engel, the president of the Chattanooga Lookouts. During the 1931 season he decided to stage a turkey dinner, but lacked the turkey. He quickly got together with Felix Hayman, who owned the Charlotte, North Carolina, team and—more importantly—a butcher shop. The result was a deal which sent Chattanooga shortstop Johnny Jones to Charlotte in return for one of Hayman's chunkier turkeys. Some famous names were pawns in those weird trades. Denton T. "Cy" Young, for instance, won more games (511) than any other pitcher in baseball history, but was so lightly regarded as a rookie that the Canton, Ohio, team peddled him to Cleveland for a suit of clothes.

Baseball's greatest star, Babe Ruth, came to the New York Yankees in a deal almost as odd. A top pitcher and outfielder with the Boston Red Sox, Ruth was traded on January 3, 1920, by the impoverished Sox for $125,000 and a personal loan of $300,000 to the Sox owner, Harry Frazee (security for the loan: Boston's Fenway Park).

Players and plots of land often were tied in during baseball's early days. In the spring of 1913, the St. Louis Browns (now the Baltimore Orioles) trained on the field of the local team in Montgomery, Alabama. When time came to break camp, the Browns found they didn't have enough money to pay the rent for the field. After some dickering, they handed over rookie Clyde "Buzzy" Wares to the Montgomery team. (Wares spent a year in Montgomery, but later came up to the big leagues for keeps.)

The Browns may have picked up that method of paying rent from the Detroit Tigers. In 1905 they trained in Augusta, Georgia, and paid their rent with pitcher Eddie Cicotte (later a star with the Chicago Black Sox).

Another great hurler, Robert Moses "Lefty" Grove, got started toward the majors by being exchanged for a center-field fence. Grove was toiling for the Martinsburg, West Virginia, club when Jack Dunn, owner of the Baltimore Orioles (then in the International League), spotted him. Dunn learned that Martinsburg owed money for the erection of an outfield fence, and offered to pay the bill in exchange for Grove. Martinsburg agreed and Grove went off to star at Baltimore, then moved up to the American League and eventually the Hall of Fame.

The strangest trades, though, have stemmed from somebody's being hungry. The Wichita Falls, Texas, team once traded Euel Moore for a plate of beans. Dallas sent Joe Martina to New Orleans for two barrels of oysters, thereby pinning the lifetime nickname of Oyster Joe on the pitcher. San Francisco shipped first baseman Jack Fenton to Memphis for a box of prunes. But when president Homer Hammond of San Antonio agreed to trade infielder Mike Dondero to Dallas for a dozen doughnuts, he managed to keep Dondero and have his doughnuts too; before signing the agreement, he ate them all up.

The hobbies of club owners also have figured in outlandish trades. Barney Burch of Omaha once gave up two players for an airplane, and Nashville's Larry Gilbert traded a set of golf clubs to land Charlie "Greek" George.

At least one owner had to trade a player to get out of a personal jam. After a convention of baseball men, a club president found himself stone broke, unable to pay even his hotel bill. He promptly went down to the lobby, which was full of club owners, and sold one of his pitchers for cash, pocketing enough to pay his bill and train fare home.

But no baseball executive ever traded more cleverly than part-player, part-owner Willis Hudlin. After pitching with Cleveland for 14 years, Hudlin became part-owner and pitcher for the Little Rock Travelers. Midway through 1944, owner Hudlin traded pitcher Hudlin to the St. Louis Browns. He pitched only two innings all season long and lost the game, but the Browns won the pennant and Hudlin got a slice of the World Series money. That winter, owner Hudlin bought back pitcher Hudlin from the Browns—and kept the change.

In 1948, I was broadcasting the Atlanta Crackers' games. Branch Rickey, then with Brooklyn, heard me and asked Earl Mann, owner of the Crackers, if he would release me from my contract.

"I'll give him to you," replied Mann, "if you give me

catcher Cliff Dapper on your Montreal farm. I want him for manager next year."

Rickey agreed, swapping a catcher for a broadcaster, and I was on my way to Brooklyn and a big league broadcasting career.

★ ★ ★

Carol "Whitey" Lockman and Hoyt Wilhelm became fast friends when they were New York Giants in the early '50s. Later they were part of a baseball trade and principals in one of the strangest coincidences in baseball lore.

In the spring of '57 Wilhelm was still with the Giants. but Lockman was an outfielder for the St. Louis Cardinals. then came a trade. The Giants, training in Phoenix, Arizona, swapped Wilhelm to the Cards in exchange for Lockman.

The Lockman family left the Card training base in St. Petersburg, Florida, and began to travel by car to the Giant camp in Phoenix. Hoyt Wilhelm and his family piled in the car in Phoenix to join his new team, the Cards in St. Pete.

Two days later the Lockmans were driving into Dallas, Texas, on U.S. 80.

"Whitey", said his wife, Shirley, "that car going the other way, that's the Wilhelms. I'd know that car anywhere. Turn around: Let's catch 'em."

Lockman made a U-turn and caught up to the car Shirley had spotted. It was the Wilhelm family all right.

The Lockmans and the Wilhelms took time out from their cross-country trips to visit with each other for half an hour. Somehow, coincidence had reached into the lives of these two friends.

★ ★ ★

You've heard the old expression, "Politics makes strange bedfellows." Well, so can a baseball trade.

Emil "Buzzie" Bavasi is retired now, but for many years he was the general manager for the Brooklyn Dodgers. John Quinn was general manager of the Milwaukee Braves, and he coveted Dodgers outfielder Andy Pafko. Andy, who grew up in Wisconsin, was a great favorite there. He had nine outstanding years with the Cubs and had finished a year and a half with Brooklyn.

Quinn came to the 1952 winter baseball meetings in Columbus, Ohio, determined to acquire Pafko from Brooklyn. He hounded Bavasi throughout the convention. After a tiresome day, Bavasi was getting ready for bed when he answered a knock on his door and found Quinn standing outside.

"We've got to talk about Pafko," Quinn told Buzzie.

"Come on in," Bavasi said. "I'm getting ready for bed."

"I'll give you $100,000 for Pafko," Quinn said.

"No deal," Bavasi said.

"How about $125,000?"

"Not enough."

Bavasi went to the bathroom, brushed his teeth. Then he put on his pajamas.

"I'll give you $150,000," Quinn told him.

"No, John," Buzzie said. "I need a player. Besides, I'm going to bed."

Bavasi hopped in the bed.

Quinn still persisted. He began to shed his clothes.

"Move over," he told Bavasi. "I'm in this bed with you until I get Pafko."

"All right, John," Buzzie said. "You give me $150,000, Roy Hartsfield, get out of my bed, and we've got a deal."

Pafko went to Milwaukee and stayed there for another seven seasons. He appeared in two World Series with the Braves, in 1957 and 1958.

Hartsfield, the player Bavasi demanded, was less successful. He never appeared in a big league game with the Dodgers. However, Hartsfield did become the first manager in Toronto history, managing the Jays from their start in 1977 through 1979.

Hartsfield and Pafko can tell their grandchildren about the time they were part of a transaction that proved that baseball trades, like politics, make strange bedfellows.

★ ★ ★

Guys get into professional baseball in many different ways. But what about the pitcher who made the majors because he was part of an expense account? That's the story of lefthander Tom Bolton.

Tom was pitching for his high school team in Antioch, Tennessee. A Red Sox scout named Fred Digby wanted to go to Nashville where he knew he could get a good deal on a new Cadillac.

Digby had heard of a high school pitcher in Nashville named Bolton, so he decided he'd buy his Cadillac and take a look at Tom. Then he could make his auto deal and put his trip on his expense account.

The scout Digby liked what he saw in Tom Bolton and the Red Sox drafted Tom as the 19th selection in the June 1980 draft.

Bolton stayed in the Boston system for $12\frac{1}{2}$ years—most of them in the minors. In mid-season of '92 he was traded to Cincinnati, and the Tigers later signed him as a free agent.

But Tom Bolton became a professional because Fred Digby wanted a Cadillac and put his car-buying trip on his expense account.

7

Fighting the Good Fight

"Sweat plus sacrifice equals success." —Charles Finley

One of the fascinating stories of the 1993 American League season was John Olerud's quest to hit .400. Even though the Toronto first baseman didn't reach that goal, he has proved himself an outstanding and bona fide big league star.

The pressure to hit .400 is awesome, but Olerud took all the attention in stride. He could put his situation in proper perspective because of a real crisis he endured in 1989. His near death at that time makes present pressures seem no more serious than an overdue parking meter.

On January 11, 1989, John was working out in the Washington State University field house. He was preparing for his junior baseball year—a season in which he was predicted to be the nation's No. 1 collegiate player.

Then, his life changed in a hurry. Olerud collapsed during that workout. Early tests were not conclusive. His father was not satisfied. His son had lost consciousness, and the father wanted answers. Six weeks later, doctors removed a hemorrhaging aneurysm from young Olerud's brain. The operation lasted six hours.

"I was scared," said the older Olerud, a dermatologist. "Being in medicine myself, I knew what might happen if John began to bleed again. The survival rate is 70 percent if the patient survives the first bleeding. But in the first two weeks after surgery, there is very often another bleeding."

So Dr. Olerud stayed by the bedside of his son and prayed.

"Baseball was the last thing I was thinking of," he said. "John was the country's best player, but I prayed only that he have a normal life. Anything more than that was just too much to hope for."

Six weeks later, John was playing baseball again. He has a metal clip in his head, and he wears a protective helmet in the field and at bat.

His dad says, "He is more at risk driving a car than he is playing baseball."

The operation brought a new perspective to young Olerud. John knows that his big league career is important, but he appreciates his astounding recovery.

"I will take things in stride now," he said. "I want to do well with my talent, and my career is important to me. But I realize that it's not the end of the world, no matter how I play."

★ ★ ★

Lou Brock, the Cardinals' Hall-of-Fame outfielder and basestealing marvel, made a contribution to the game that has had more long-lasting effect than his famous non-slide in the '68 World Series against the Tigers.

After the 1968 World Series, Brock went with the Cardinals to Japan. He watched Sadaharu Oh hit some tremendous home runs and asked him to give him one of his bats. Oh was kind enough to oblige.

The bat was different. It was cupped at the end of the barrel where the wood had been hollowed out to take the weight from the end and give the bat true balance.

Brock tried the new bat and liked it. The next year, he began to use the Oh bat in the National League. It worked well for him. There were some protests at first. But the bat was legal, as long as it was made from only one piece of wood.

Brock had only a few models of the Oh bat and had a hard time keeping them. He'd be careful after a time at bat and always tossed the bat to a batboy. Otherwise, someone might steal it.

When he got his 3,000th hit, he was using the cupped bat. Now, between one-third and one-half of the big leaguers use that kind of bat.

The ironic twist about the cupped bat is that it originated in America. The Japanese copied it. Around 1910, the Savannah Bat Company manufactured what was called the teacup model. It was similar to the cupped bat we have today. Nobody paid much attention to it. Somehow, years later, the Japanese ran across the teacup and from it designed their own version.

Who first came up with the teacup idea? I don't know, but since the Savannah Bat Company was located in Georgia, I have a strong feeling it might have been Ty Cobb.

★ ★ ★

In everybody's life, the first time has special meaning. It might be the first kiss, the first job, or even the first time at bat in the major leagues.

I've talked to several major leaguers and former major leaguers about their debuts. The most interesting story came from former Pirate Richie Hebner. I'll let Richie tell about his first:

"It's September 1968, and I've just reported to the Pittsburgh Pirates. We're playing the Reds at Forbes Field. Jim Maloney is pitching for the Reds, and he is Red hot. He's struck out 15 of our guys. We're in the eighth inning and I'm watching in awe from the bench.

"Manny Jimenez comes to bat for us. There are two out. Freddie Patek is on first, and we're losing, 1-0. Maloney zips a fastball past Jimenez and the umpire says, 'Strike one.' Manny turns around and squawks—in Spanish. Here comes the next pitch. Strike two. Jimenez protests again in Spanish.

"The ump knows exactly what Manny is saying and throws him out of the game. Our manager, Larry Shepard, needs a pinch-hitter for Jimenez. We've got three rookies on the bench, Al Oliver, Manny Sanguillen, and me. Shepard looks over the bench. Now, I didn't go to school just to eat lunch, so I'm hiding behind the water cooler. No way I want to face Maloney—especially with two strikes on me.

"But Shepard finds me.

"'Get a bat,' he says, 'and go up there and hit, Hebner.'

"Remember, there are two out and Patek on first. Two strikes on me.

"I dig in against the great Maloney. His first pitch to me is a pitchout. Patek breaks for second. Johnny Bench guns him down. The inning is over. So is my phantom time at bat. I go back to the dugout.

"'Hey,' I tell the guys. 'He's gotten 15 strikeouts, but he didn't get me.'

"That was my first at-bat in the big leagues, but I really didn't bat at all.

"A couple of days later, against the Cubs at Wrigley Field, I had my first genuine time at bat. I faced Fergie Jenkins and flied out to right field."

★ ★ ★

John Smoltz was destined to be a Tiger. His grandfather worked on the Tiger Stadium ground crew. And as a Lansing sandlotter, John dreamed of the day when he would pitch for the Tigers.

He signed with Detroit on September 22, 1985, and began to pursue that dream. Then came the shock of his base-ball life on August 12, 1987.

"I was in the dugout at Glens Falls," he recalled. "Somebody handed me two notes. One said, 'Urgent. Call your father.' The other said to call Tiger Stadium."

John called his dad first.

"Have you heard?" his father asked.

"No, what?"

"You've been traded to Atlanta. I saw it on the news."

"I couldn't believe it," John said. "My dream of pitching for the Tigers was over. I called Tiger Stadium and Dave Miller confirmed the trade. Detroit was swapping me for Doyle Alexander. The Braves wanted me to report immediately to Richmond."

It was a good break for Smoltz. He had been struggling at Double-A Glens Falls at 4-10 and couldn't find himself.

"Detroit had only one roving pitching coach in the whole organization," John said. "Our team would see him only twice a year. I was confused and needed help. The Braves sent me to the Instructional League. They had three pitching coaches there working with me one-on-one. The Tigers had always concentrated on my mechanics. The Atlanta coaches, especially Leo Mazzone, downplayed mechanics and zeroed in on perfecting my various pitches. They taught me to relax."

Smoltz had a great 1988 season at Triple-A Richmond. He was 10-5 when he was called up. At 21, he was now a big leaguer, but not with his dream team.

Since he was seven, Smoltz had loved the Tigers. He heard all their games on the radio. His dad and brothers would drive from Lansing to Tiger Stadium. His grandfather would interrupt his ground-crew duty, grab John by the hand, and introduce him to Bill Lajoie and Jim Campbell.

"Someday," his grandfather would say, "this young man will be pitching for you guys."

Campbell and Lajoie had heard that boast from many

relatives about many youngsters, but this time it almost came true.

Smoltz was an outstanding pitcher at Waverly High in Lansing. He starred in the Stan Musial League and the Junior Olympics. Yet most big league clubs bypassed him. "They were scared off by my decision to enroll at Michigan State," Smoltz said. "I already registered, but decided not to go at the last minute."

He was a Tiger for three years until the Alexander trade. Now, he is an established star with Atlanta. A few years ago, Smoltz struggled but found himself after consulting sports psychologist Jack Llewellyn.

"He became a close friend and confidant," Smoltz said. "He taught me some basic precepts—especially positive visualization. He helped me relieve my tension."

As a member of the Braves' outstanding rotation, Smoltz looks forward to another pennant and the thrill of another World Series.

But he will never forget August 12, 1987, and the trade that changed the career of a young pitcher who had seemed destined to be a Tiger.

★ ★ ★

In a hot midwestern summer in the early '70s, Frank Tanana was an overrated, overpaid, lonely rookie with a sore arm. Today he is an established 20-year big league star.

Frank almost didn't make it through that miserable 1971 season at Idaho Falls.

As a youngster in Detroit, he had dreamed of pitching for the Tigers. He was an outstanding schoolboy pitcher and big league scouts put him at the top of their lists. However, he hurt his arm while pitching for Catholic Central in his senior season.

"I tried to throw side-arm without being properly warmed up," Frank recalls. "Something popped. I began

to favor that arm and got tendinitis in my left shoulder."
He kept trying to pitch. He even pitched in the Catholic
finals in Detroit against Holy Redeemer. His arm hurt so
much he had to leave the game after four innings.
Tigers scouts and others sighed and scratched Tanana
off their lists. But one scout—Carl Ackerman of the California Angels—stood firm. Ackerman had seen the young
phenom fan 32 in a regional tournament at Cincinnati. On
his recommendation, California made Tanana its first-draft
pick and gave him a $50,000 bonus.
Frank reported to Idaho Falls to begin his career—with
a sore arm.
"I can't pitch. I have a bad arm," he told manager Bob
Clear. Clear shook his head, wondering what to do with a
17-year-old rookie pitcher who couldn't pitch.
When the bad news reached Anaheim, the Angels dis-
patched Ackerman to Idaho Falls to determine whether this
sore-armed lefthander was the same sensation he had
signed. Ackerman urged the Angels not to give up on his
prize prospect. Tanana went to California, where Dr. Frank
Jobe examined him and told him the only cure would be
complete rest for his ailing arm.
Frank was miserable. He had rejected a Duke basketball scholarship, and now his baseball career appeared to be
over before it had even begun. He appeared in one game
that season—as a pinch-runner.
His teammates resented him. On long bus trips the
$50,000 wonder was an easy target. "He's useless." "He's
replacing somebody who could help us." "We don't need
him."
Such abuse was so scathing on one trip that team leader
Darrell Darrow intervened.
"Lay off the kid," he shouted. "It's not Frank's fault.
Someday his arm won't be sore, and he'll be a big leaguer.
Give him a chance."
From then on, Tanana's rookie season was bearable.

After a winter of rest, the arm recovered, and Frank began his march to the majors.

★ ★ ★

Heroes don't always get the treatment they deserve. Take the case of Carlton Fisk. Carlton's final year with the Chicago White Sox was fraught with bitterness. The Chicago management released the future Hall-of-Famer in the middle of the 1993 season. When Fisk tried to enter Comiskey Park to watch the American League playoffs, he was turned away.

But even in the most heroic moment of his career, Fisk found himself unappreciated. It was after the sixth game of the 1975 World Series. Fisk's dramatic 12th-inning home run had beaten the Reds. You've all seen the TV replay—Fisk, prancing along the first-base line with outstretched arms, coaxing the ball to stay fair. Fisk was the Hero of the World. "What excitement," he recalled. "There was all kinds of attention. The press—radio and TV—kept me up late at the park. I finally had to pull away. My family was waiting.

"It was strange, but I had no place to spend the night. I had been renting a house in Belmont, Massachusetts, but the lease expired at the end of the season. We expected to get a hotel for the family.

"I got in the car, and I packed in my wife and two kids. We drove all over Boston looking for a hotel vacancy. Finally, the only solution was to drive two-and-a-half hours to our home in New Hampshire and spend the night there. It was almost daylight by the time we got there.

"After a short and restless night, I drove back to Fenway for the final game of the Series. Needless to say, I was not too alert for the seventh game."

Ironic, isn't it, that after that historic home run, Carlton Fisk couldn't find a place to spend the night?

★ ★ ★

Baseball tempers typically flare late in the season. I can tell you about a famous fracas, because I was there. The confrontation proved to me that any time a player wants to fight, he can do it without one of those "Don't hold me—let me at him" situations.

It was September 6, 1953, and the Dodgers were running away with the pennant. They were in front by 11 games. When they came to the Polo Grounds that afternoon for their final game with the Giants, they had beaten their hated rivals nine straight games.

In the second inning, after a two-run homer by Roy Campanella, Giants pitcher Ruben Gomez hit Dodger Carl Furillo on the left wrist with a fastball. After a few harsh words, Carl was standing on first base. Suddenly, he bolted toward the Giants' dugout. As he raced over, he ran straight toward Giants manager Leo Durocher.

Leo and a small group of players rose to meet the on-charging Furillo. Carl grabbed Leo in a headlock and threw him to the ground. Somebody stepped on Furillo's hand, spiking him.

The umpires ejected both principals from the game. A reporter asked Furillo, "Why would you be foolish enough to go into the Giants' dugout and challenge Durocher and all those players? Didn't you realize you were outnumbered?"

"He made them throw at me once too often," Furillo said. "I told you I'd get him."

"But what about knowing all those guys would gang up on you?"

"Didn't worry me," Furillo answered. "A lot of those Giants hate Leo, too."

Carl came out of the melee with broken bones in his left hand; he missed 22 of the Dodgers' 154 games. But his enforced rest assured him the National League batting title;

his .344 average was two points better than St. Louis' Red Schoendienst. Stan Musial finished third (.337).

In the World Series against the Yankees, Furillo appeared in all six games and batted .333, but the Dodgers were beaten by the Yankees in six games. How much difference a healthy Carl would have made in the final result is something we will never know. He certainly never backed down from anybody—not even Leo Durocher.

Umpires might have hated Durocher more than rival players. After the Furillo incident, a reporter asked Bill Engle, who was umpiring at first base, "Why didn't some Giant player tag Furillo with the ball when he had left first base to battle Durocher?"

"Oh, nobody could do that," he answered. "I had called time so Carl could go get him."

★ ★ ★

The ambition of every pitcher is to win 20 games in a big league season.

In his first year with the Yankees, the Hall-of-Famer Waite Hoyt won 19 games. He missed number 20 because of his teammate and close pal, Babe Ruth.

The Yankees had clinched their first pennant early in 1921 and were playing out the string—readying themselves for the World Series with the Giants. In a final tuneup, Hoyt started against the Philadelphia Athletics. For seven innings he blanked the A's, 7-0.

In the dugout, manager Miller Huggins summoned Hoyt.

"Waite," he said, "we've got this game in the bag. The fans here want to see Babe Ruth pitch. He hasn't pitched all year and it would be a treat for them. You can take the rest of the day off."

Ruth came in to pitch. The Athletics rallied for seven runs and tied the game. Since the result was meaningless,

Huggins allowed Ruth to continue on the mound. In the ninth, Ruth homered, and the New Yorkers won the game, 8-7.

The Babe was the winning pitcher, despite giving up seven runs. The starter, Hoyt, had pitched seven scoreless innings. His 20th victory was almost in his grasp, but the impulsive, fan-pleasing move by Manager Huggins denied him his goal.

Hoyt was a great pitcher, but he did not reach the 20-win plateau until the banner Yankee year of 1927, when he won 22. He went on to pitch 21 years in the major leagues, winning a total of 237 games. In 1969 Hoyt was inducted into the Baseball Hall of Fame.

His fondest memories were his pitching days with the championship Yankees. As a broadcaster, Hoyt told many stories about those Yankee days, emphasizing the greatness of his close friend Babe Ruth.

Yet, he never forgave the Babe for cheating him out of his chance to win 20 for that very first time.

★ ★ ★

Somewhere among the thousands of big league managers and players there may have been a man as blunt as the late Rogers Hornsby. But, if there has been such a man, I never met him—or even heard about him.

Hornsby, I knew. And I was very fond of him. I knew him best when he managed the Cincinnati team in 1952 and 1953. I was broadcasting the Giants games those two seasons.

Although Rog was blunt and considered by many to be uncommunicative, I found him easy to talk to...easy to talk to on one condition—that your subject was baseball. I'd sit with him in dugouts or hotel lobbies and listen to him talk baseball. Change the subject on him and he'd grunt and move away, or just sit and remain silent.

He acted the same way on the field. If one of Hornsby's pitchers was faltering, he wouldn't walk to the mound to talk and bring in the relief man. No sir, he'd merely get up from his dugout seat, look toward the bullpen, and wave for the new man to come in.

Hornsby didn't smoke, drink, or lie. He faced the facts. No off-the-record stuff for Rog. He let his words fall where they may. Once on Chicago TV, Rog was being interviewed by Jack Brickhouse.

"Say, Rog," Jack said, "you've been out in Oklahoma. Did you see my good friend Grayle Howlett out that way?"

"Yes, I did," Hornsby answered. "I don't like him."

Once, a Brooklyn writer approached Hornsby for an appraisal of the Boston Braves, a team he was playing with that season.

"They tell me," the writer said, "that this team has a good shot at the first division."

"With what?" was Rog's retort. "These humpty-dumpties can't win for losing."

Hornsby's bluntness lost him many a job. The Giants let him go after he had feuded with one of John McGraw's favorites, Fred Lindstrom. He was winning a pennant for the Cubs in 1932 when he was released.

Some of the owners he worked for didn't like the idea that Rog bet the horses. If they asked him if he was betting the nags, he always answered that he was. Others did their betting in secret. Not Rog. He was open about everything. When he managed the Baltimore Orioles in the International League, Rog even had a tout travel with him. He wasn't satisfied to get his tips over the phone. He had to have them right with him, in person. Come to think of it, horses was one of the few subjects other than baseball that attracted Mr. Hornsby's attention—and his money, too. But it was clearly an exception.

Tom Meany once told a story about how Hornsby's interest was centered on baseball. Back in the mid-'30s

Hornsby was thumbing through the *Chicago Daily News*. It was a Saturday night edition and the pages were filled with reports of the Army-Notre Dame game in New York. There were stories on Wisconsin-Purdue, Northwestern-Minnesota, Pitt-Nebraska, Illinois-Ohio State, and even Chicago and Beloit. There were photos, charts, play-by-play, and color stories.

The sports section ran eight pages. Rog looked up one column and down the next, searching for an item about baseball. But he had no success.

"You know," he told his companion, "there's nothing in the sports pages, is there?"

That was Rog. The blunt Mr. Hornsby.

8

Treating 'em Lightly

"You gotta be a man to play baseball for a living, but you gotta have a lot of little boy in you, too."—Roy Campanella

One of the worst hitters of all time was the angular left-handed pitcher, Hank Aguirre. For Aguirre even to meet the ball caused more surprise than Smokey the Bear starting a forest fire.

Hank spent 10 of his 16 years in the majors with Detroit. One afternoon in the late '60s at Yankee Stadium, Hank hit a drive to deep right center and slid safely into third base.

After he had gotten to his feet and dusted himself off, Aguirre turned to Detroit third base coach Tony Cuccinello and asked: "Now, Tony, shall I steal home?"

"Are you kidding?" asked Cuccinello. "It took you eight years to get this far, Hank. Don't spoil it now."

★ ★ ★

In show business if you have a name that's hard to say or hard to remember, you change it. It happens in baseball, too—especially with a very long name. Such was the case of Antonio Vincent Bordetzki, a native of Remus, Michigan. A name like that probably would end up in a boxscore as BDTZKI, or some such alphabetical horror. In fact, that was just about the information imparted by a sportswriter to Mr. Bordetzki when he first broke into baseball. The sportswriter told him: "It doesn't really make much difference what you change it to, but be sure to make it brief."

And so Bordetzki took that advice to the letter. He went into the major league record books as Bunny Brief.

Incidentally, Brief went on to play quite a while in the minors and had two "brief" seasons with the St. Louis Browns and one each with the Chicago White Sox and the Pirates.

★ ★ ★

Earl Averill, one-time Cleveland slugger of the 1930s, had been in a dreadful slump for two weeks. In situations such as that, batters get desperate. They'll try anything. So will general managers who are trying to help them. That's how Billy Evans, the Cleveland general manager, happened to listen to the inebriated chemist.

The test-tube expert was a rabid Cleveland fan. In fact, he seemed to have just two loves in his life, the Indians and alcohol. He concentrated on the Indians each afternoon and spent his evenings thoughtfully draining the cup that cheers. Neither qualification is generally accepted as a forceful recommendation for an expert on batting techniques. But Evans was desperate, as was said before, and he was willing to listen to anyone.

"Averill's swingin' the wrong kind of bat," said the chemist to Billy. "I can get him out of his slump. Not enough hittin' surface, that's his trouble. Lemme have some of his bats. I'll fix 'em."

Evans shrugged his shoulders. After all, what could he lose? "What's the matter with the hitting surface?" he asked.

"Not hard enough," snapped the chemist. So Billy ordered that a batch of the Averill models be turned over to the chemist. The chemist disappeared for a few days and returned with the bats. They now had a dark brown band around them, about seven inches wide at that point hitters refer to as "the fat part of the bat." Evans was suspicious, and he knew that the umpires would be suspicious as soon as they saw them. "We've got to do something to these," he remarked. So he summoned Lefty Weisman, the Cleveland trainer. "Lefty," he said, "I want you to take these bats and stain them a dark brown so that this band won't be noticeable." By game time they were ready.

Then Billy called the slumping Averill aside. "Earl," he announced, "here are the bats you need. You don't have to hit the ball hard. Just meet it and the ball will ride a mile."

The big slugger was not too convinced. But his first trip to the plate did the convincing. He ducked away from an inside curve, falling back from the pitch. The ball accidentally nicked the extra special bat and shot in a line to the outfield. It was a base hit beyond question. Averill got the idea very rapidly and "the old confideence"—as Jesse Burkett used to call it—filled him with a happy glow. In his next 30 times at bat, the big fellow slashed out 15 hits and averaged better than two bases a hit.

But Evans grew more and more worried. That crazy chemist, he was convinced, had done more than use a chemical preparation on the bats. He must have loaded them with steel rods. The bats must be illegal. Anxiously he called the trusty Weisman to his office. "Lefty," he said solemnly, "whenever Averill's bat breaks, I want you to rush out and gather up every piece before anyone else can pick them up. If you're away from home, send the pieces to me airmail. If you're at home, bring them to my office."

Finally a bat broke. Lefty swooped out of the dugout and gathered up the pieces as though they were diamonds.

Instantly he rushed them to Evans' office and Billy sent for a carpenter. "Saw this bat, inch by inch," ordered Billy. In fear and trepidation, he waited for the ominous crunch of steel blade striking steel rod.

The carpenter sawed through the first segment cleanly. Then the second. And the third and so on. The bat was cut into one-inch pieces—and there was nothing there but solid wood. Billy breathed a tremendous sign of relief and sent for the inebriated chemist, who was slightly more inebriated than usual as a result of the Averill hitting streak.

Evans ordered the same chemical treatment for all the Indian bats. But the chemist, completely vague about the entire operation, had forgotten the secret formula he'd used on the Averill bats. He never was able to duplicate it.

However, drunk or not, the chemist did accomplish one thing—he got slugger Earl Averill out of one of the worst batting slumps of his career.

★ ★ ★

In the mid-1920s the Yankees were the most powerful hitting club in all of baseball. They were the window breakers, and many a game they won with their late-inning home run attack.

When Earle Combs came to the club from the minors, his reputation was that of a fine basestealer. And when he reported, he told the Yankee manager Miller Huggins, "Down in Louisville where I played I was so fast they called me the mail carrier."

But Huggins was a sharp little man, and he had a quick answer.

He said, "Well, son, I tell you: Up here we got Babe Ruth and some other big guys who hit the ball all the way out of the ballpark. We don't need basestealers. If you get on base, just wait there and they'll get you in. Yes, up here we won't call you the mail carrier, we'll call you the waiter."

★ ★ ★

Cynics have often argued against spring training, contending that its only value is in publicity. They claim that the grind is too long, and that almost any player can get in shape in two weeks. Also, they cite that a long training season is an open invitation to injuries.

But spring training has always been with us. It's a tradition. The custom started in the 1870s and first gained notoriety through a trip made by the old Chicago White Stockings. That club won the pennant in the summer of 1885, and the beer that winter had been so good that their chests had slipped and their legs had become watery. So manager Cap Anson took them all to Hot Springs, Arkansas. There they boiled the brew out of their flabby carcasses and put resilience into their underpinnings.

Part of the tradition of spring training is its literature. Some of the yarns are strictly legend. Some really happened.

Frank Frisch was nearing the end of his playing career in the mid-'30s and still managing the Cards. In spring drills, the aging and aching Mr. Frisch boiled over when he saw young Sam Narron in a corner of the field, leaning lazily on his bat. Frank let out a verbal blast which had even the veterans turning around.

"What the hell are you doing?" he asked Narron.

"It's this way, Mr. Frisch," the rookie answered. "In the clubhouse this morning you told us young players to pick out a star on the team and imitate him in everything he did..."

"Well?" growled Frisch.

"Well, sir, I picked you."

★ ★ ★

One of the toughest umpire-baiters among recent baseball managers was Eddie Stanky. Ed could be scathing and sarcastic with the umpires. When he was managing the St. Louis Cardinals, Stanky had an interesting set-to with umpire Augie Donatelli.

Wally Moon, Card batter, took a called third strike and put up an argument with Donatelli. Stanky then came out of the dugout but never spoke to the ump. He said to Moon, "Wally, don't argue with this ump. He is the most courageous, honest, sincere, and accurate umpire in baseball. Don't argue with him."

Stanky started to the dugout, then turned around and yelled at Donatelli. "That was not a strike and you know it."

"Lovely speech, Ed," Donatelli answered, "but one sentence too long. You're outa' the game!"

★ ★ ★

Big league managers get asked questions wherever they go. Writers, announcers, and fans all bombard them with questions. Back in the 1930s, Jimmy Dykes was manager of the poor Chicago White Sox. The Sox were short in the win column and also short in the financial department.

Well, Jimmy went to church and the pastor, during the collection, had a question. "Jim," he asked, "why did the Sox sell Al Simmons to Detroit for $75,000?"

Well, Jimmy didn't answer. He just smiled. After the service he went to the pastor, and here's what he told him: "I'm sorry that I couldn't answer that question you asked me during the church service, but now I can, and let me try to put it this way: The White Sox sold Al Simmons to Detroit for the very same reason you were taking up that collection in church. We need the money."

9

In the Line (Off) Duty

"It took me 17 years to get 3,000 hits in baseball. I did it in one afternoon on the golf course."—Henry Aaron

Johnny Berardino spent 11 years in the major leagues as a utility infielder. His top thrill was playing for the American League champion Cleveland Indians in 1948.

However, his real ambition—even while he was in the majors—was to be an actor. John was born in Los Angeles and as a youngster had appeared in a few of the "Our Gang" comedies. After he became a baseball professional, he augmented his income by working in baseball movies. He also did theater at the Pasadena Playhouse.

Breaking into the theater and movies was not easy for Berardino. He was considered an athlete and only a part-time actor. One of John's first important auditions came when he had a tryout for a part in *The Stratton Story*. This was the film which starred Jimmy Stewart as Monty Stratton, the White Sox hurler who had lost a leg in a hunting accident.

Sam Wood was the film's director. He called together a

group of actors who were to play the roles of ballplayers in the film.

"He gave me the quick brush-off," Berardino recalls. "He never heard of me and said I didn't look like a major league ballplayer."

Maybe Johnny looked more like a doctor. He later became famous in television, playing the role of Dr. Steve Hardy for more than 25 years on the popular soap opera "General Hospital."

★ ★ ★

It was Dwight Eisenhower's lifelong secret that he was the only professional baseball player among all the U.S. Presidents. Had he not kept that secret in his West Point days, he would not have become the great military leader of World War II and President.

Dwight's first baseball experience came as a center fielder for his Abilene, Kansas, high school team. In 1911, in his first year at West Point, he played both baseball and football. The next fall, playing football for Army against the Carlisle Indian School, Ike injured his knee and never again played football.

He continued with baseball but failed to make the team at West Point.

"Not making that Army team was one of the great disappointments of my life," Ike once said.

Now about that secret of Ike's. Before he even went to college, he had played professionally.

"I needed money to go to college," he said, "and the best way to get it was to play pro baseball. I didn't do very well at it, but playing pro ball did help me with my financial problems."

While still at West Point, Eisenhower played professional ball one summer in the Kansas State League under the name of Wilson.

Many college athletes in those days competed in pro sports under assumed names—even though the NCAA rules forbade such activity, and the penalties were stiff. There were even more serious rules at West Point, where student-athletes had to sign a pledge that they had never competed in pro sports. Ike signed that pledge—a clear violation of the West Point honor code. Any cadet who violated the honor code was expelled.

An expelled Eisenhower might have changed the course of world history; Ike would never have become a general. There would have been no Eisenhower, the World War II hero, and he would never have become President of the United States.

In their excellent book, *Baseball: The President's Game*, William B. Mead and Paul Dickson point out that Ike revealed that he played pro ball when interviewed in June 1945, after his return from Europe. However, after that year, he became much more careful about his secret and instructed his staff to maintain a silence about his baseball career.

The authors write that "playing a few professional ballgames certainly was no sin. But under the rules of the day, it could have cost Dwight David Eisenhower his place in history."

★ ★ ★

The best-looking women in town are always the wives of the baseball stars—you can bet on that. So it should come as no surprise that ballplayers' wives have often modeled and appeared in TV commercials.

But long before the advent of the TV commercial, the Tigers had a handsome pitcher whose wife not only was a model—she was the Sun-Maid Raisin Girl. If you saw a Sun-Maid Raisin box—in New York or Boston or Berlin or Istanbul—the face on that box belonged to this lady.

The pitcher was Earl Whitehill, and his wife was named Violet—Violet Oliver, before she married Whitehill.

Violet had been a chorus girl on Broadway (where she met Earl) and Miss California. As the Sun-Maid Raisin Girl, she toured the United States and even met President Woodrow Wilson.

I had heard for many years that Earl Whitehill's wife had been the Sun-Maid Raisin Girl, but it was one of those pieces of trivia that floated around, and nobody could ever trace the truth of it. Then one night in Anaheim, the Tigers were playing the Angels, and into our radio booth walked Vince Desmond, then the Tigers' traveling secretary.

"I left some tickets for Mrs. Earl Whitehill tonight," he told me. "She is coming to the game with Tommy Bridges' widow. They both work in a nursing home near Anaheim."

I asked Vince to go to Mrs. Whitehill's seat and ask whether she really was the Sun-Maid Raisin Girl. He came back an inning later with the news that Violet's picture was indeed the one we had seen on the Sun-Maid Raisin box. But, he added, there had been other Sun-Maid Raisin Girls. Mrs. Whitehill had been pictured on the boxes for many years. But two or three ladies had followed her.

What about her ballplaying husband? Earl Whitehill was one of the most handsome major leaguers. He never worked as a model, but he was a fine left-handed pitcher, winning 218 games over his 17-year career. Earl started in the majors with the Tigers and pitched for them from 1923 until he was traded to Washington after the '32 season. In 1933 Whitehill pitched the Senators to a pennant with 22 wins and shut out the Giants in the World Series for Washington's only victory against the New Yorkers. In the late '30s, he pitched for Cleveland and for the Cubs.

Whitehill was tough and never backed down on the diamond. Once he protested an umpire's decision by heaving the ump's whisk broom over the grandstand. Another time, after a tough loss, he locked himself in his hotel room and wouldn't let his roommate in.

Off the field, Earl was handsome, cultured, and polished. He and Violet were quite a couple. She took quite a picture, and the record book tells us Whitehill was quite a pitcher.

★ ★ ★

Baseball remembers Hugh Casey as the Brooklyn pitcher whose pitch eluded catcher Mickey Owen and made Owen the goat of the 1941 World Series.

I remember Casey as a big boisterous guy with a cigar in one hand and a scotch in the other. Casey was also the reason for my only deep-sea fishing trip.

Late in 1948 the Dodgers had finished a night game with the Phils in Philadelphia. Casey suggested to Brooklyn rookies Carl Erskine, George Shuba, and me that we go deep-sea fishing the next day.

"We'll go out for a little while and have some fun," he told us. We agreed to meet him at Sheepshead Bay and make the trip.

After I got back from Philly, I had only a couple of hours of sleep. We met at the docks around 8:30 that morning and sailed away.

I don't remember what I had for breakfast (probably a hot dog and orange juice), but it began to regurgitate as soon as we were out on the ocean. I was feeling woozy.

I looked at Shuba and Erskine. They weren't feeling any better than I was. The sun came up and began to bear down on us. We felt worse and worse as the day wore on.

We tried to fish, but our luck was no better than our health.

Meanwhile Big Casey was having a great time. He was laughing and joking and had no trace of seasickness. He kept puffing on a big, black cigar and sipping whiskey.

Erskine, Shuba, and I were dying a slow death. I wanted to go ashore, but wouldn't dare suggest it. I'm sure the other two felt the same way, but they also kept their mouths shut.

Casey was the only one interested in fishing. In the late afternoon he finally landed a blue marlin and hauled it in. There were cheers from the crew and from Shuba, Erskine, and me.

The day wore on and we got sicker. Finally, Hugh decided to bring the boat in. We docked about 8 or 9 P.M. and headed back to Brooklyn.

"Hey, you guys," Casey said. "If any of you want that marlin, I'll give it to you."

"Thanks, Hugh," Erskine told him. "You caught the fish. It should be yours. Besides, you've got a restaurant here in Brooklyn where you can put that marlin on display."

I don't know how Shuba felt about that, but I was in full agreement. I had no place to put a marlin and certainly didn't want any reminder of my only venture into deep-sea fishing.

The next year Casey drifted to Pittsburgh and then the Yankees. After that, he was through.

I missed him in 1949, my second year with the Dodgers. I had ridden to Ebbets Field every day with Hugh and manager Burt Shotton, and Casey was always kind and friendly.

Hugh and I went back a long way together. Like me, he had grown up in Atlanta, and I followed him even in his sandlot days. After the 1941 World Series I did a long *Sporting News* story about a special celebration Hugh's hometown of Buckhead, Georgia, staged for him. At that dinner, Casey showed his true character. The Buckhead Elks presented Hugh with a fine shotgun. And there were various wisecracks about Casey using the shotgun on Mickey Owen. Casey didn't like the remarks and said so.

"You folks have got Mickey Owen wrong," he said. "He is always hustling and there is not a man on our team who blamed him for missing that third strike."

In finding that quote from Casey, I had to check my *Sporting News* article of November 6, 1941. When I reread the piece and looked at the pictures, I couldn't help but notice an ironic twist to the story.

Near the bottom of the page is a one-column photo of Hugh and his wife, Kathleen. A caption said: "Mrs. Hugh Casey was one of the interested spectators when her hubby who pitches for the Brooklyn Dodgers was honored by the Elks of Buckhead, Georgia, Hugh's native heath. Casey, an inveterate hunter during the off-season, was given a costly shotgun by the Elks. He is shown here with Mrs. Casey, an enthusiastic out-of-door woman, displaying the weapon."

Ten years after that article appeared, Hugh Casey phoned his estranged wife from an Atlanta hotel room and told her he was going to kill himself.

He took that same favorite shotgun, stuck the barrel in his mouth, and pulled the trigger.

I still remember him on that fishing trip. Hugh Casey with his big black cigar and his bottle of whiskey.

★ ★ ★

His name was Stanley Burrell. He used to bring us the lineups in the radio booth at the Oakland County Coliseum. They called him Hammer because he looked like Henry Aaron. He wore a green and gold baseball cap with VP on it.

Indeed, Athletics owner Charlie Finley even introduced Stanley as his vice president at a press conference. Finley had discovered Burrell in the Coliseum parking lot, pitching pennies and dancing around with his teenage pals. Stanley's brothers worked in the A's clubhouse, so he was always hanging around.

When Stanley joined forces with Finley, the Oakland franchise was in bad condition. The team had slipped in the standings and Finley's visits became less frequent: He continued to run the Athletics and his insurance company from Chicago.

Only a few relatives remained in Oakland to man the front office. There were no full-time scouts. And the team's radio rights were passed off to a small University of California radio station in Berkeley.

At $7.50 a game, Stanley Burrell became a part of this scene. When Finley needed to follow the A's games from Chicago, Stan phoned him the play-by-play. The Hammer even talked himself into the radio booth a couple of times and did his own play-by-play. That career came to an abrupt halt when the station's general manager tuned in his car radio.

"Get that kid off the air," he ordered.

Hammer had other ideas of self-promotion. He went to Frank Cienscyk, the A's equipment manager, and told him, "Mr. Finley wants me in an A's uniform with a hammer on the back."

"When Charlie calls me and tells me that, you'll have the uniform," Cienscyk told him.

The players looked on Stanley as a spy. "It was scary," says Steve McCatty, who was pitching for the A's at that time.

"We'd look up at the pressbox, see Hammer on the phone, and realize that our careers might depend on what a teenage kid was telling Finley back in Chicago."

Let's press the fast-forward button to 1990.

It's Game Three of the American League playoffs. On the mound to throw out the ceremonial first pitch is Stan Burrell, the Hammer. Except now he's known as M.C. Hammer, superstar of the music world.

He's M.C. Hammer, Grammy winner, seller of seven million-plus albums, rap artist, and multimillionaire.

But he couldn't have made it to the cover of *Rolling Stone* without the A's. First Finley discovered him, then two Oakland players provided him with seed money for his record company.

Now Stanley Burrell, the A's former vice president, is on top of the world.

And where is Finley?

Charlie is out of baseball, but still working. Recently he was in Europe negotiating a deal for the production of M.C. Hammer watches.

★ ★ ★

When Denny McLain pitched for the Tigers in the mid-'60s, he roomed with shortstop Ray Oyler. One night in Boston, Denny, who was to pitch the next afternoon, went to bed early. Oyler was still out on the town.

Denny woke up the next morning and went to the bathroom to insert his contact lenses. They were no longer in the glass of water where he always kept them. He looked around the bathroom for the lenses, but couldn't find them.

McLain shook his roommate and woke him.

"Ray," he said, "have you seen my contacts? They were in the bathroom last night."

"Naw, I haven't seen 'em."

"Ray," said Denny, "did you get up in the night and drink a glass of water?"

"Yeah, I did," Ray answered.

It was obvious that Ray Oyler had swallowed McLain's contact lenses. The next question was how they could retrieve the lenses.

Denny solved the problem. With an approach that combined practicality and philosophy, McLain told himself, "This too shall pass."

The roommates recovered the lenses, and Denny pitched that afternoon at Fenway Park, his contacts intact.

★ ★ ★

Ryne Duren has become a part of baseball lore. He was never a great pitcher, though he did have a few brief moments of glory. But his legacy to baseball was that of the prototype wild pitcher. He was the "Wild Thing" long before the song, the movie, or the '93 Phillie Mitch Williams made that designation famous.

I knew Ryne in his first big league season. He was with the Orioles when they came into the American League in 1954. His blazing fastball and his poor vision combined to make him the game's most feared pitcher.

He would squint through his thick glasses and then throw his first warm-up toss onto the screen high behind the plate.

He reached his heights with the Yankees in 1958. He was brilliant in the World Series, winning a game, saving another, and turning in a 1.93 ERA.

His relief effectiveness continued into 1959, but after that he faded quickly. Hard drinking took its toll. But he fought back from decline and despair and finally beat his worst enemy, alcoholism.

I saw Ryne recently in Florida. He is now a happy man. He still wears those thick glasses, and he loves to laugh at himself.

He told me that several years ago he was driving in his home state of Wisconsin when a big truck rumbled past. The truck was from Alberta, Canada, and had the driver's name, Ryne, on the door.

Duran contacted the trucker on his CB.

"Hey, you trucker with Ryne on the door, talk to me," he said.

"OK, what do you want?"

"Where'd you get that name?" Ryne asked him.

"My dad named me after some no-good ballplayer nobody ever heard of," the trucker answered.

"That guy was me," Ryne told him. "Let's stop at that cafe down the road and have a cup of coffee."

★ ★ ★

Has anybody seen a life-size statue of Ty Cobb any-where around Detroit? That statue must be around some-where, but it's been missing since shortly after its creation more than 65 years ago.

After the great Ty Cobb left the Tigers, he came back to play against Detroit as a member of the Philadelphia A's. His fame was so great that the people of Detroit tendered to Ty a testimonial luncheon.

Praise overflowed, and in the enthusiasm of the mo-ment, someone proposed that a life-size statue of the hero be executed and placed where it would inspire the youth of Detroit.

The next morning at his hotel, Mr. Cobb had a caller— a Russian wearing a beard. He announced that he was the appointed sculptor of the Cobb statue. He asked Cobb to strike a pose, and he went to work.

Cobb fell in with the idea of the statue. Moreover, he signed hotel checks for the artist's refreshments during the making of the little clay model. Later, he was astounded to find out that the man with the beard lived on a diet of strawberries and cream — and the price of the tabs reflected his taste. It was said that the bill for the one-man straw-berry festival was as imposing as Cobb's lifetime batting average. Ty paid the bill and left town with a lighter pock-etbook, resolving to have nothing more to do with art in general and with bearded Russian sculptors in particular.

After Ty and his team had departed, the sculptor went to work on the life-size model of Cobb in his studio. 'Tis said that an umpire was called in to give his opinion of the completed model. When he saw the statue, he quivered with rage and was about to attack it. "That's Cobb, all right," he shouted and leaped through an open window into the backyard.

Finally, the sculptor called on Detroit mayor John W. Smith to announce that the statue was finished.

"What statue?" the mayor asked.

"The statue of Ty Cobb," the sculptor answered.

Well, after the big luncheon, the mayor had forgotten all about the statue and had assumed that everybody else had, too. They all had, except for the sculptor.

"I'm to get $20,000 for this statue," the sculptor said.

"I congratulate you," said the mayor.

"Who's going to pay me?" asked the Russian.

"I hope you find out," said Mayor Smith, politely.

Not all the detectives in Detroit could discover who really had ordered that statue of Ty Cobb. And nobody was willing to pay. The statue languished for months in the artist's studio. Then both statue and sculptor disappeared. Where they went, nobody knows.

So if you run across a statue of Ty Cobb, don't be reluctant to speak up. Probably by now someone's paid for it.

William Earnest Harwell at age eight.

Harwell as sports director at WSB-Atlanta in 1940.

Atlanta Crackers broadcaster Ernie Harwell (center) interviews Mobile manager Pancho Snyder (left) and Crackers' skipper Kiki Cuyler (right).

With the Polo Grounds in the background, the New York Giants'
broadcasting team of Russ Hodges and Ernie Harwell pose in 1950.

Harwell in a pre-game chat with Mr. October—Reggie Jackson.

Broadcaster/song-writer Harwell presents Detroit pitching ace, Denny McLain, with the music to "Maestro of the Mound," a tune cowritten by Harwell and Tony Aquino.

A visit with Willie Mays at the All-Star Game in Detroit, July 13, 1971.

Hall of Fame honors. Ernie Harwell, after receiving the Ford Frick Award, addresses the crowd gathered at Cooperstown, New York, in August 1981. (Photo: Richard Collins)

A Hall of Fame portrait: the three 1981 inductees—Al Kaline (left), Ernie Harwell (center), and Charlie Gehringer (right).

Harwell, on one of his many visits to the White House, presents President Ronald Reagan with a copy of his first book, *Tuned to Baseball*.

Harwell with longtime friend and broadcast partner Paul Carey in the booth at Tiger Stadium.

Two familiar faces: Tiger manager Sparky Anderson and Harwell.

Two fan favorites—Tigers slugger Cecil Fielder and the Voice of the Tigers.

Ernie with his favorite teammate, Lulu, his wife of 53 years.

10

Out of the Mouths…

"Say this much for big league baseball—it is beyond any question the greatest conversation piece invented in America."—Bruce Catton

Author's Note: The following are selected excerpts from on-the-air radio interviews I conducted with assorted baseball personalities over my 46-year big league career.

FRED LIEB ON BABE RUTH

Harwell: *Fred, you covered the Yankees for the papers throughout the career of Babe Ruth while he was with the Yanks. What kind of a fellow was Babe Ruth?*
Lieb: Well, Babe was really a pretty nice guy. He was certainly a rough character and certainly wasn't a cultured, cultivated man, and things happened to Babe Ruth I don't think could have happened to any other individual. Once, when Babe's career was at its height, a Columbia professor made a study of him. When measuring his reactions in 25 different categories, he found that Babe was either 1, 2, or 3 out of the average 100 men. He called him "a man in a million."

Harwell: *Now what about Babe and his so-called feud with Lou Gehrig? Was that an actuality?*
Lieb: Yes, it was. It really started between their wives. They went on a trip to Japan together. Lou had gone on an earlier trip that I promoted with Herb Hunter in 1931, and he had such a grand time that he just begged Yankees owner Jacob Ruppert to let him go on another trip after he had gotten married. Eleanor, Gehrig's wife, and Claire, Babe's wife, had some misunderstanding or something. And then, of course, the feud spread to the husbands. I guess they didn't speak for a half-dozen years or so—until that last great performance they put on for Gehrig, New York's tribute to perhaps its greatest sports hero.

Harwell: *What about Babe Ruth's relations with the other players on the Yankees. Were they good?*
Lieb: Well, they were good if he had any relations with them at all. Of course, he always had a certain little squad that often were bachelors and kind of ran wild. But as far as Babe's relations with others in the club, well, we had a pitcher by the name of Charlie Devens, if you remember back that far. He was a Harvard man. In St. Louis, instead of taking the train from the station right in the city, we'd often go to a place called Dinwar or Duwar. It was probably about five miles outside the St. Louis city limits. The players would gather there, maybe one or two, three or four. When I got there this one time, this Charlie Devens was sitting there. Probably five or seven minutes before the train was scheduled to start, Babe came along. Charlie Devens was kind of sitting alongside me. Babe said to me, "Is that guy with us?" And I said, "Well, I guess he should be. He's pitched in about a half-dozen games." "Oh," he said, "Yeah, that's the guy. We don't make many runs for him do we?"

FRED LIEB ON TY COBB

Harwell: *Here's Mr. Fred Lieb, a veteran baseball writer who*

covered baseball all but six years of Ty Cobb's long career with the Tigers and with the Philadelphia Athletics. Fred, do you consider Cobb the best player you ever saw?
Lieb: Well, I used to, and it sort of got me into a little jam with my publisher out in St. Louis, Taylor Spink, because he had me write one side of an article, "Ruth versus Cobb." H.G. Salsinger of Detroit, of course, took Ty Cobb's side, and I took Babe's. The issue was good for about five articles in *The Sporting News*: Why Salsinger thought Cobb was best, and why I thought Ruth was greatest. When I first agreed to write this article, I told Spink, "Well, I don't really think Ruth *is* the greatest, I think Cobb is." He said, "Oh, you know more about Ruth than most any other guy that's writing there. So you write it. You can certainly put in a good argument for Babe's side." So I did, and I think I told a pretty good story. But in the bigger sense of the word "great," I think that Ruth was greater because his accomplishments were far greater. By that, I mean the impression he left on the game; he changed baseball entirely around. And the fact that he was known all over the world. I remember when it was rumored that he died—when he had that "stomach ache heard around the world." That was 1925. Well, an English paper, a London paper, had a two-column story on Babe's death, and when somebody showed that to me, I said well he really is world famous if a London newspaper writes a two-column obituary on him. There were a great many mistakes in the obit that they got perhaps from some American journalist in London, but it did show that Ruth was not only a great American sports hero, but the greatest among those who never took particularly kindly to baseball. They didn't know he didn't die until about 20 years afterwards.

Harwell: *Was Ty Cobb as mean as a lot of people said he was?*
Lieb: I think he was. He was one of the cruelest men I've ever known. There were some reasons for it. There was a

tragedy in his family. His mother shot his father, and he was very devoted to his father. It was something like Gehrig's mother-and-son complex. Well, Cobb's father was a big man in his life. He never wanted to do anything that would displease his father. I'm not criticizing him now as a man, because he certainly had many good qualities about him, but Cobb had a streak of cruelty that ran through him. I think he would spike some players deliberately, though his own shins had rows of slits where players had indented into the bone with their spikes. I wasn't a witness to this, but baseball writers quite frequently were invited to Dover Hall, a hunting lodge, near Brunswick, Georgia. They were sitting outside, chatting, talking baseball or something like that, and all of a sudden a dog, a small hound, climbed up on this porch and Cobb got up and kicked this dog, probably kicked him about 30 feet away, like somebody would kick a football. It wasn't just a friendly kick off the porch. And he says, "That damn dog should know better. That's a working dog, and this porch is only for house dogs." Well, he could have killed that dog. And there were some other things about Cobb from my long contact with him. I know he was a mean man.

TED WILLIAMS ON HITTING

Harwell: *Here's Hall-of-Famer, Ted Williams. Ted, Babe Ruth had his pitching nemesis, Hub Pruett. Did you ever have one? Anybody ever get you out in the big leagues with any regularity?*
Williams: Well, that's the difference between he and I. He only had one, and I had an awful lot of them. It would take me a long time to tell you. There's probably 20 pitchers that I could name that were really tough. And it wasn't a matter of striking out, but I never could get ahold of their ball consistently as well as some of the others.

Harwell: *Any special type pitcher, a guy that was effective…*

Williams: No, it was a funny thing. In my book that I wrote on hitting, I mentioned five pitchers in the book. One was a cute little lefthander, kept it outside, breaking stuff. Another one was a knuckleball pitcher. And another had a sinking fastball that I could never quite get ahold of. I would think that a hard sinking-ball pitcher day in and day out was toughest. And a knuckleballer.

Harwell: *What was the hardest pitch for you to hit?*
Williams: A good, hard, quick breaking ball is a tougher pitch to hit than the fastest fastball. For me it was.

Harwell: *What's the biggest mistake that most young hitters make when they come to the major leagues?*
Williams: Well, here's a funny thing: I saw a shot of the three outstanding pitchers last year. One was the rookie pitcher, one was the Cy Young winner, and one was something else special. They showed a picture of each pitching, just a little insert of pitching. All of them threw the ball in the dirt, and the hitters swung at every damn one of them. So getting a good ball to hit is all important, because I couldn't have hit some of the pitches they were swinging at.

Harwell: *Of all the guys you've talked to about hitting, was there any one particular guy that helped you the most?*
Williams: Well, of all the many hitters in my life, great hitters ahead of me, that I thought could say something that just might trigger something, I thought Hornsby gave me probably the greatest single advice: "You got to get a good ball to hit." I can't hit that one up here, high, and I can't hit low and away off the plate, and I can't hit a ball that fools me. So getting a good ball to hit means all that; a ball in a good spot, a ball that doesn't fool you. Then, there's the time when you have to concede to the pitcher, when you say, "I got two strikes, I got to do something a little quicker, a little tightening up, choke up an inch." That's probably the best advice...that and don't try to pull the ball.

Harwell: *How about ballparks? You liked Detroit, didn't you?*
Williams: I loved Detroit, but you know it's a funny thing. They had a challenging type of pitching staff there. They had guys that always thought they could get you out, and they were more challenging than they should have been with me at times, I thought. And still, I went to other parks, like Yankee Stadium, and boy, they didn't ever give in to me. They were always out there, out wide. If he gets it, he's going to swing, you're going to hit at that, or he ain't going to swing. And I walked more times in Yankee Stadium than any other ballpark. I had an inviting park in Detroit, and I got enough pitches that I hit well there.

Harwell: *What about Fenway?*
Williams: Fenway had one great advantage for me. We had a right-hand-hitting club and still a long right-field fence. And they said, well geez, it's a matter of pitching to him with a long right field or pitching these other guys out in short left field, so I got a lot more chances to hit there, at times. And I felt I hit better in Fenway than in any other park. I hit .333 on the road, I hit .360-something in Boston.

AL LOPEZ ON CATCHING

Harwell: *Here's the Hall-of-Fame catcher and manager, Al Lopez. What do you look for when you want to check out a catcher? What's good and what's bad about a catcher in his fielding performance?*
Lopez: Well, Ernie, first thing you'd naturally look at is what kind of a thrower he is. Although they didn't run as much in the old days as they do today, I think you better have one now that can really throw, because if not, I think you're going to lose a lot of ballgames. But, you also need a guy that can handle the pitchers. A catcher to me is like a quarterback on a football team. He's got the whole ballgame in front of him, and he's calling all signs. He's on

every pitch. He's got to be able to receive the ball. I think they average more passed balls today, and I think it's the one-handed gloves. One catcher averaged more passed balls today than the whole league when I was catching. I went one year with no passed balls and the following year with one passed ball. I also think they lose a lot of strikes by catching one-handed. We were taught to catch everything two-handed and to bring everything to the center of the plate, right into our body. A good receiver, a guy that's smart, tries to help the pitcher out. A good catcher, in my opinion, is the guy that can kind of read the pitcher's mind and make him comfortable with what he's calling for. If the pitcher thinks that you're a dumb catcher, he's going to have to worry about what you're calling for and also worry about trying to get the hitter off. But when he has confidence in the catcher, all he has to worry about is getting the hitter off.

Harwell: *What's the ideal position for a catcher? I mean, you see a lot guys down in the dirt now. Do you like that, or would you rather see a guy up a little bit?*

Lopez: No, I don't think he should be down in the dirt. I know one catcher in the National League, I don't want to mention his name, but he used to sit down on the ground, and I don't see how he could get up to field a ball if they happen to bunt it to either side. I think he should stand up, be in position. Naturally, if there's nobody on base he can stay on his haunches trying to get the pitcher to pitch down, but I think he should be up at all times and ready to go in case of a bunt or a swinging bunt so he can go out there and field the ball.

Harwell: *Now it's proverbial that catchers are slow runners. Do some of them start out fast and get slow because of the position that they have to get into, or are they just put there because they're slow?*

Lopez: That's part of it. If they're slow with a good arm and big, they might be put there. In the olden days, even before my time, a guy like Ray Schalk was about the only small man who was a catcher. Muddy Ruel was another one. Then I came along. I wasn't big. I think they began to look for quicker guys with a good arm. But in the olden days, they didn't have this obstruction rule that they have now. They used to block the plate without the ball, and you had a terrible time trying to get into the plate. So, especially early on, size in a catcher helped. They'd block the plate, and unless you bowled them over, you weren't about to get in. Now they call it obstruction.

SHIRLEY POVICH ON WALTER JOHNSON

Harwell: *He's been one of our outstanding baseball writers over many years. He was writing in the mid-'20s and he continues to write into the '90s: Shirley Povich, from Washington. Shirley, I know that you were a boy reporter when Walter Johnson was pitching for the Senators. Tell us a little bit about Walter. What kind of person was he?*

Povich: Well, outside of being the great pitcher that he was, Walter Johnson was probably the most modest ballplayer I have ever known. And he had a humility that was truly outstanding. One time, however, he did surprise me. I invited him after his retirement to see Bob Feller pitch for the first time. He saw Feller the first inning and said, "My he's fast." Second inning, he says, "He's awful fast." I popped the question to him by the fourth inning when he had warmed up: "Tell me, Walter, what do you think? Is he as fast as you?" And Johnson startled me. He said, "No." And in his slow way he added, "I don't think he is as fast as Grove. This young fellow has got a great advantage. I used to give them a good look at the ball." Johnson, you know, was a side-armer. "This boy has got an advantage," Johnson said. "He pitches out of his shirt. This is a big difference." He admired Feller but his honesty collided with his modesty, and I guess his integrity won.

Harwell: *Shirley, could Walter Johnson have been even better if he were a little meaner or would it have made that much difference?*
Povich: Oh, I think he could have, yes. If he had been a meaner pitcher, he'd have put better figures up there. Ty Cobb told me, for example, "I knew Walter was afraid of hitting me with a pitched ball because when he did, everybody in the park gasped. I used to take advantage of this timidity by crowding the plate and hitting his outside pitch." But Walter was a trusting sort. I did see him hit Eddie Collins one day in the leg or the knee or wherever, and Collins went down and the whole park was fearful: My God, what happened to Eddie Collins? Walter Johnson was the first one to rush in...Collins was on the ground, and there he is writhing, but ultimately he got up, in great applause now, because he has decided to continue the game. Then Collins steals second on the next pitch! So Walter was a little bit gullible.

Harwell: *Now did Walter Johnson have long arms and sort of a girlish kind of an arm? I've always heard that.*
Povich: Yes, he did. It was evident when he walked...long arms like a gorilla that hung down almost below his knees. He got the leverage out of the long arms. I was startled the first time I saw him because not only was he pitching sidearm, but he was actually a little bit underneath. And he was a contradiction to the belief that all righthanders, fastballers, should come overhand. He did give the players a good look at the ball. I will say one more thing about him, Ernie. On the day when his 16-game consecutive winning streak was broken, he was charged with a run as a relief pitcher when he came in and the man on second scored. The president of the American League ruled that Johnson was responsible for a run that was on second when he came into the game. Quite unfair.

MONTE IRVIN ON WILLIE MAYS

Harwell: *Here's Hall-of-Famer Monte Irvin. Good to see you again, Monte.*
Irvin: Always good to see you, Ernie.

Harwell: *You and Willie Mays had a special relationship. You were the first guy that he saw when he came to the Giants, weren't you?*
Irvin: That's right. I can remember it as if it were yesterday, when he came to us in Philadelphia, May of 1951. He's fine looking, robust. You know, he wasn't that big, but you could tell that he was a natural, particularly when he got dressed and went out on the field, and started to throw the ball around. You could see it in the way he handled himself, in the way he threw the ball, in the way he caught the ball. He had flair, and he had style; he carried that through all of his career.

Harwell: *He had a bad start though, and you were one of the guys that helped him out through that bad start. Tell us about that.*
Irvin: I think he went to the plate maybe 15, 16 times during that series with the Phillies and got no base hits. I remember after the last game in Philadelphia, Durocher came over to him and put his arm around him and said, "Now, listen, Willie, you're my center fielder." He said, "Don't worry about not getting any hits. The hits will come. We got guys like Bobby Thomson and Wes Westrum and the rest of the guys to hit the home runs. So you just catch the ball and throw, and field the ball and run the bases the way I know you can, because you're going to be my center fielder." The next night, on a Friday, we opened at the Polo Grounds. First time up against Warren Spahn, Warren threw Willie a change-up, and he hit it over that left-field roof for a home run. And I talked to Warren the other day, and he said, "He hit other home runs off me, but never on a change of pace."

Harwell: *Did Willie calm down after a while? Did he relax a little bit?*

Irvin: Yes, he did. He was a little nervous because he was totally brand new. He was just a youngster from Birmingham, Alabama. But after we talked about the weaknesses and strengths of the pitchers and what to expect in certain situations, he learned real fast. He and I got into a controversy about that last game, the one where Bobby Thomson hit the home run, the playoff against the Dodgers. Willie said if they had walked Bobby Thomson, he thought that Leo (Durocher) might have pinch-hit for him. And I said, no way. I said, remember he told you that he's going to sink or swim with you, and if they had walked Bobby Thomson, you were going to be the hitter. I'm sure of that. But Bobby hit the home run, Willie never had to come to the plate, and it got me off the hook because I had made the only out in that inning. And so, with one swing of the bat, Bobby made it all right for both of us.

Harwell: *When Willie came back from the service, he was bigger. He was stronger. I guess he was more mature, wasn't he?*

Irvin: More confident. He developed the basket catch, and you could tell that he had matured. He was more worldly. He had kind of grown up, found out what the world's about and so I just knew that he was going to have the year that he did. I think he was the Most Valuable Player that year. He was just outstanding. He did everything very well, and we were just delighted to have him back.

YOGI BERRA ON CATCHING

Harwell: *Our guest is Yogi Berra. Yogi, what about all these Yogi Berra stories? Some of them are true, some of them aren't. How did all that get started?*

Berra: Well, I don't know. I think everybody when they go to the banquets, they always mention my name on it. You know, "Yogi said this, he said that." I guess the one you could really get the truth on is Joe Garagiola, because you know we grew up together. We known each other a long time. He got a pretty good idea.

Harwell: *Well, Yogi, if you said all those things they say you said, you wouldn't be doing anything but talking all your life, would you?*
Berra: You're not kidding. That's the truth. I don't know. Sometimes I say it, you know, I'm home, my kids, my wife. I'll say something, and they'll say, "There's another one." And I say, "What'd I say?" But usually I don't. I didn't say all them things. Some are true, and like you said, some are false.

Harwell: *What do you think Yogi Berra would have done if he hadn't have been a big league ballplayer? What kind of business would you have been in?*
Berra: My gosh, I don't know. I couldn't tell you, Ernie. I know I worked in a shoe factory when I was a kid before I started playing ball, and maybe I might have stuck with the shoe factory, I don't know.

Harwell: *Now you've been a player, you've been a coach, you've been a manager. Which is the most fun in the big leagues? Playing?*
Berra: Playing is the best fun. Coaching is too. You know, you see these kids. You get some good ones, make you happy and everything. I enjoy this. This is my 41st year now, Ernie, and I still enjoy it. I think, if I didn't want to do it, I don't have to do it, but I like it. I can't wait till spring training comes along.

Harwell: *What's the kick out of coaching? Seeing young kids develop?*
Berra: Right. You know, help out the kids, the young catchers and everything. That is good, to see some young kids come along.

Harwell: *Yogi, what's the most important thing a young catcher has to learn when he comes to the big leagues?*

Berra: Boy, I know they're hard to find now, Ernie. I know that. We're looking one over ourselves, and I don't know. I think the kids just don't want to do it no more. They don't want to work hard enough for it. And I always tried to tell them, it's the best position to play. You have a lot of fun. You get to talk to everybody up there. You're in the game more and everything.

Harwell: *What's the secret of throwing as a catcher, getting the ball off quick?*

Berra: Well, I see a lot of kids today, Ernie. They seem like they catch the ball first and then they throw it. I always liked to go up for the ball, like an infielder, and throw it. I liked to move with my right foot first into the ball, and then you put something on it. A lot of catchers catch it, and then they throw it. They do all their movements after they catch the ball, instead of doing it while the ball's in flight. Lot of times, they say, "Well, the hitter's going to hit me." You know, fights start. And I try to teach them you won't get hit. I let them swing enough so you won't hit me. But it's tough to do, for some of them. I don't know, like Dickey when he got ahold of me, my gosh, he worked my butt off every day. So you get used to it. You know, I used to go home after workouts, stand in front of a mirror, work on my footwork, just to see how I was doing.

Harwell: *Well, it paid off for you.*

Berra: Oh, I loved it. I owe everything to Bill Dickey.

PETE ROSE ON WINNING

Harwell: *Well, if there was ever a man to be a cinch for the Hall of Fame, he's the guy we're talking to right now, Pete Rose. Pete, of all the things you've done in baseball, what do you think you'd like baseball to remember you by?*

Rose: Well, Ernie, it seems like people remember you for things that happen on national TV. Probably the '73 playoffs when I had the collision at second base with Bud Harrelson, the '70 All-Star Game when I had the collision with Ray Fosse. But there again, I played a long time and I got a lot of base hits, and I think I'm proudest of the fact I played more winning games than anybody in the history of baseball. Because, I think, all I ever tried to do as a player was to get base hits, score runs, and win games. And I played more winning games and got more base hits and I'm fourth in runs scored, so I guess two out of three isn't bad.

Harwell: *When you beat Ty Cobb's record, when you surpassed 4,000 hits, everybody was rooting for you, unlike when Hank Aaron was chasing Babe Ruth. Do you think there was any reason for that?*
Rose: Well, I think probably because when people started writing about Ty Cobb, they wrote about how nasty he was and how tough of a player he was, and I think people sort of resented that somewhat, the modern-day fans. But when everybody started writing about Henry Aaron, they also wrote positively about Babe Ruth. See, I think Babe Ruth's the greatest player that's ever played the game of baseball. That's my own personal opinion, because I think Babe Ruth did something no other player's been asked to do, and that is he saved baseball. Back in the '20s and early '30s, when he used to go into a town, he saved that franchise because of the attendance they had for the three games that Babe played in. And it enabled baseball to grow. And I think all of us as baseball players, or as announcers doing baseball games, should really thank Babe Ruth for everything he contributed to baseball.

Harwell: *What's the best thing about baseball as far as Pete Rose is concerned?*
Rose: Winning. I think the best thing is winning, and the

worst thing is losing. All my ups and downs are either winning the World Series or losing the World Series, or winning playoffs or losing playoffs. My biggest up was '75 when we won the World Series for the first time; my biggest down was in '70 when we lost the World Series, '72 when we lost the World Series to Oakland, '73 when we lost the playoffs to the Mets, and in '83 when we lost the World Series to Baltimore.

Harwell: *When you were growing up, as a kid, did you ever dream that you'd break all these records?*
Rose: No, I never dreamed anything like that. You dream about being a big league baseball player. I used to go to Crosley Field every night when I was a kid to watch the Reds play. And that was, I think, the dream of every young kid, to be a baseball player, and I just happened to grow up in Cincinnati. So I wanted to be a Cincinnati Red baseball player. But even when you become a big league baseball player, I don't think you ever dream about records. If you get lucky, the most important thing about being a baseball player is to make the big leagues. And when you make the big leagues and you get lucky enough to make an All-Star team or hit .300 or win a batting title, then you sort of set standards that you try to accomplish every year. And the first thing you know, you go 20 years and you're pretty, relatively healthy, and the records will all pile up.

Harwell: *Pete Rose, we thank you for being our guest.*
Rose: Well, thank you, Ernie. And best of luck to Sparky and his boys because Sparky's the best manager I ever played for, and I played for 11 of them.

GEORGE BRETT ON .400

Harwell: *Here is George Brett of the Kansas City Royals. Do you remember your first game in the big leagues?*

Brett: Yeah, it was 1973, May 3, against the Chicago White Sox in Comiskey Park. I faced Stan Bahnsen. We ended up winning the ballgame. And my first pitch I saw, I hit a line drive and Stan Bahnsen kind of just reacted. And my next at-bat, I hit a broken-bat single to left, and then I was on my way.

Harwell: *Did you feel a little nervous? Were the knees "a-knocking" slightly when you were up there for the first time?*
Brett: Scared to death. Paul Schaal, the third baseman for the Royals, had just sprained his ankle, and I remember my manager, Harry Malmberg, down in Omaha, came over to my apartment and said, "Hey, you're going to the big leagues." And I thought he was talking to my roommate, Mark Littell. And I said, "Hey, that's great, Mark. Go get 'em." And the next thing I know, he said, "No, you, George." So I went down to the ballpark, got my stuff real quick, went to the airport, and he told me not to worry. I wasn't going to be playing. I got there, and batting practice was in progress. I walked into the locker room, my first big league locker room as a player, and saw my name on the lineup card, and all of a sudden I started getting nervous. I went out there. I went 1-for-4 that day, 1-for-4 the next day in Minnesota, then I sat on the bench for two weeks. Then when Paul was ready to play again, I was back down to the minor leagues. But I was brought back up later that season, didn't play much, and then in 1974 I was the last player cut out of camp. And they traded Paul Schaal beginning of April, or the end of April, brought me back up, and I've been here. This is my 15th year.

Harwell: *George Brett, you've come as close as anybody to hitting .400 in the last few years. Can it be done, or is it too tough? What's the story on hitting .400?*
Brett: Well, obviously you got to get a lot of hits. Nineteen-eighty was the year I hit .390; I missed it by five hits. And I

went over the .400 mark with six weeks to go in the season. At that time, everybody started asking me about it, and I laughed. I thought it was funny. Little did I know, with two weeks to go in the season, I would still be over .400. I had one good week and one bad week. The bad week came with two weeks to go. I got down to .384, and then all of a sudden I figured I couldn't do it. So I was able to relax a little bit more then. I ended up having a great last week, hit over .500, brought the average back up to .390. But I think it can be done. If I came five hits from it, I think there's a lot of better hitters in the league than I am right now. Wade Boggs obviously, Don Mattingly. There's a lot of guys that I think are capable of doing it, but what they have to do is just kind of put the pressure aside and go out there and just play their game. With two weeks to go in the season, I went out and tried to hit .400, and all of a sudden I couldn't do it, but for the month that I was over .400, I was just having fun. I was just going out there, and I was very selective with the pitches I swung at. With two weeks to go, I started letting the pressure get to me, and all of a sudden found it real tough to get a hit. Someone's going to do it someday. I just hope I'm around to see it.

Harwell: *Is most of the pressure in that situation from the media?*
Brett: All the pressure is from the media. It was very easy for me to relax during the game, but before and after the game was very tough on me. I really think I let it affect me a little bit, not that much, but if I'm fortunate enough to stay with my good fundamentals and have another run at it, I think I'd be better prepared for it this time around.

FRANK ROBINSON ON HIS START

Harwell: *Frank Robinson, the manager of the Baltimore Orioles, I want to talk about your early days in baseball. What about your big league debut, do you recall that?*

Robinson: I recall it. It was in Cincinnati in 1956 against the Cardinals, and Vinegar Mizell was the pitcher. And first time up I hit a double off the center-field wall. Next time up I hit a single, and I got an intentional walk in that ballgame. But we lost it, 4-2. Stan Musial hit a two-run homer, I think it was in about the eighth inning, and they beat us on opening day.

Harwell: *Well that's quite a tribute, when a rookie gets an intentional walk.*

Robinson: Yeah, I think it went to my head, too, because after the game they asked me the difference between major league pitching and minor league pitching, and I said there was no difference, it was all the same. Then after that I proceeded to go 0-for-3.

Harwell: *What about when you first came into baseball, in the minor leagues, your debut. Do you remember that?*
Robinson: I remember that. First time up I hit a triple off the left center-field wall, and the next day I hit a home run over the same spot in that ballpark. It was 353 feet down the left-field line in Ogden, Utah, so it was a big minor league ballpark.

Harwell: *Who was your first manager in the minor leagues?*
Robinson: My first manager was Earl Brucker, and the team when I joined it in June after coming out of high school, was already in first place. They were on a roll, and I think we wound up winning the league by 12 games. It was a good experience being on a winning ball club the first time in professional baseball.

Harwell: *How many of those guys on that first team made it to the major leagues?*
Robinson: One.

Harwell: *Frank Robinson.*
Robinson: That was it.

Harwell: *How about some of the managers you've played for?*
Who was the first manager in the major leagues you played for?
Robinson: Birdie Tebbetts was my first manager, and I
thank him for that this day. And I will always thank him,
because without Birdie being a fatherly figure and understanding young ballplayers, I don't think I would have
stayed up with the major league ball club after the start I got
off to. I think I'd have been back in the minor leagues. But
he stuck with me, explained things to me, sat me down for
one day when I was struggling, and told me why he was
doing it, and then put me back in the lineup the next day,
and my season took off.

Harwell: *How about your teammates? Who were the guys that*
helped you along the most on that Cincinnati team?
Robinson: Well, actually they all did. They made it very
easy for me getting into that big lineup with Ted
Kluszewski, Wally Post, Gus Bell, Ed Bailey, guys like that,
Johnny Temple. I just was one of the players, just fit right
in. Nobody paid any attention to a young rookie; they were
concentrating on these veteran players so much that they
didn't pay any attention to me, and it made it much easier
for me on the ball club. But a player who helped me defen-
sively, and I had trouble in the outfield when I first came up
with the terraces in Cincinnati, was Hal Jeffcoat, who had
been converted from an outfielder to a pitcher. He would
take me out every day and hit flyballs for 15 minutes, on his
own. No one told him to do it. And it just made me a better outfielder, and I really appreciated that.

WADE BOGGS ON HITTING

Harwell: *Well, here's the hitting machine himself, Mr. Wade*
Boggs. You're not playing tonight, I hear.

Boggs: No, I'm not. The reason that I played last night was to try and get the 200 hits in front of the home crowd. I should have taken last night off, but I was fortunate enough to get the two hits, so I think the rest will do me good tonight.

Harwell: *How did you hurt that knee?*
Boggs: I slid into third base, trying for a triple the first game that Detroit was in town, and I slid wrong and hyperflexed my knee, or whatever you call it. It just bent the knee back the wrong way. And as it turned out, I strained some ligaments in there, and it really didn't feel too good last night trying for that double.

Harwell: *What is the most important asset you have to have to be a good hitter?*
Boggs: I think it's patience and discipline, both of those have a lot to do with it, because in this league they try to get you out with off-speed stuff. And they're not going to give you a good pitch to hit, as Sparky's featured in the past.

Harwell: *Well you're an excellent strike-two hitter. You're conscious of that, I'm sure.*
Boggs: That's what I take pride in because I work the count to my favor, and usually it goes to two strikes, and most of my hits come with two strikes.

Harwell: *Now after you foul off those pitches, do you finally get the pitch you want?*
Boggs: More than likely. The more pitches you see in an at-bat, the better your chances of getting a hit.

Harwell: *What about the routine of a pitcher, his pattern? Can you figure that out pretty easily?*
Boggs: Really, they don't set patterns with Wade Boggs. They mix it up, mix it in, mix it out, off-speed stuff, breaking balls.

Harwell: *So you just look for whatever comes up there.*
Boggs: I just see it when it comes out of the hand and don't commit too early. And once I do that, most of the time I've got a pitch to hit.

Harwell: *What about your work ethic? I know you've made yourself a fine defensive third baseman by working hard. Do you work just as hard on that as you do your hitting?*
Boggs: I have to work a little bit harder on my defense. It doesn't come as natural as the hitting does, and it takes a little extra work, but it's something that I take a lot of pride in—the ability to improve my fielding the way that I have.

Harwell: *Well I've read that you even improved your running skills a couple of years ago. Is that true?*
Boggs: When I first came up to the big leagues, I was with a track coach in the off-season. And he found out that I wasn't running on the balls of my feet. And once I started running on the balls of my feet, it made me a little bit quicker.

Harwell: *Wade, why was it you weren't drafted fairly high?*
Boggs: Well I was drafted in the seventh round by Boston in '76, and I thought I'd go higher than that because of the years that I had in high school. And I was just fortunate enough to be with Boston. I've been with them ever since.

Harwell: *Has it been a good club for you?*
Boggs: Most definitely. As a matter of a fact, Fenway's built for me.

Harwell: *Now you've got more home run power than you've ever had. Is that a conscious effort with you?*
Boggs: It's not conscious. It's just something that happened this year, and I knew it would take a few years to do it. It took George Brett, I think, 4 years to hit 20 home runs. And it was just something that took gradual progress, and once it came around, so far I've got 24.

Harwell: *Is this a matter of technique or is it just maturing or growing stronger?*
Boggs: I think it's a little bit of everything wound up together.   I lifted a little harder this past winter, and I've changed my technique a little bit to get balls up into the air. And I just think everything worked in my favor.

Harwell: *Well the good thing about it, it hasn't bothered your percentage at all either.*
Boggs: No, not at all. That was one thing that I was worried about. If I started hitting more home runs, I thought the average would suffer. It hasn't.

JOE DIMAGGIO ON STREAK ENDING

Harwell: *It's a pleasure to chat with Joe DiMaggio. Joe, you were so famous as a player, did you ever have any privacy at all?*
DiMaggio: Of course, you're pretty well protected. When you're playing the World Series, you're generally around a crowd of people, your own group. You're all housed in pretty much the same place, but on the road . . . you're pretty much left alone. My roommate was pitcher Lefty Gomez, and of course he did a great job of screening things. And it wasn't the fault of the fans—they were just well-wishers. At times they would come knocking on the door about 2 or 3 o'clock in the morning, just wanting an autograph, to say hello, things of that sort. And of course we had other people that wanted you to go to banquets or luncheons and breakfasts, you know all those kinds of things. I would have to say that was the pressure. Now the thing that I did to escape most of all of that was to come to the ballpark about four hours early. There was nobody at the park at that time, and I just hung around the ballpark.

Harwell: *Is it true that when you were coming to the park in Cleveland on the day the streak was broken that the cab driver said that he thought the streak would be broken?*

DiMaggio: Gee, I thought all that stuff was forgotten. That's the truth, and I was riding along with Gomez at the time. The cabbie just had the feeling, he says. He turned around and says, "Joe, I just have a feeling that tonight is going to be the night that they're going to break your streak." And Gomez, I recall, just jumped all over him, and he kind of felt miserable about it because he told me later on, "You know, that bothered me throughout the whole ballgame."

Harwell: *The streak was broken, but you started a brand new one, didn't you?*

DiMaggio: That is correct, but I must give a little credit where it's due. One of the great third basemen is the one who really stopped it. Kenny Keltner made two fantastic plays. He played along the line and made the long throws that just nipped me, bang bang. But it had to come to an end some time.

Show Time

11

Another Opener, Another Show

"All beginnings are somewhat strange; but we must have patience, and little by little, we shall find things, which at first were obscure, becoming clear." —St. Vincent de Paul

Opening day is my favorite day of the year. It's a glorious combination of Christmas, Easter, and the Fourth of July.

• Christmas: Baseball opening its presents.

• Easter: Baseball's birth of spring with some fans, like some churchgoers, showing up for only that one time in the year.

• Fourth of July: Baseball's celebration, a civic event of sportanic fireworks.

I've seen all kinds of openers: 80-degree weather and in the snow; tight pitching duels and one-sided fiascos; long, slow games and close, exciting ones. I've seen enough of them to predict what might happen on a typical opening day. Something like:

• The first group of fans in the stadium will be the bleacherites. At least six of them—despite near-freezing weather—will not be wearing shirts.

• The rookie pitcher for the home team will report late because he couldn't find the ballpark.

• The uniforms will be cleaner. The grass will be greener.

• Outside the park, radio music from the blaring loud-speakers will be louder than cheers later in the game.

• Three fans who drove from Kentucky to the game will get beery happy in the bar across the street and never see the game.

• The boxseats, where local society reigns, will be filled last.

• The governor and the mayor will be booed with equal volume and intensity.

• A 35-year-old businessman who played high school baseball with the visitors' superstar will try to find him and relive old times. He'll be rebuffed by ushers behind the dugout.

• The pressbox will overflow with writers who won't return to the stadium for the rest of the season.

• "TV Live at Noon" will interview the groundskeeper.

• The first loud cheer will be for the fan who catches the first foul. He will be from Muskegon.

• A rookie will get the home team's first hit. In two weeks, he'll be in the minors.

• Four loud and abusive fans will threaten to sue when the concessionaire refuses to serve them more beer.

• In the eighth inning, there will be an announcement in the pressbox that the press elevator is out of order.

• After the game, the losing manager will say: "It's only one game. We'll be ready again tomorrow."

• The winning manager will say: "It's only one game, but it's great to get off to a winning start."

• A fan who's seen 52 straight openers will leave the park, saying, "It's still fun. There's nothing like opening day."

★ ★ ★

The thrill of opening day means a lot to everybody in baseball. And throughout the history of the game, openers have produced added highlights on the diamond itself. Sometimes these highlights reflect a super effort by some great star. Sometimes they are weird, crazy kinds of doings. In 1913 when the Brooklyn Dodgers christened the new Ebbets Field, officials started to open the bleachers and found they had lost the key. And, when all the dignitaries made the march to center field for the flag-raising, they discovered there was no flag to raise.

Flag trouble also vexed the New York Giants when they opened the 1928 season against the Boston Braves. As Mayor Jimmy Walker and 30,000 fans looked on, the flag was raised—upside down.

The Giants had another unfortunate experience: It snowed all night before their 1907 opener. But, despite six inches of snow, they refused to postpone the game. By the time the eighth inning rolled around, they were losing to the Phils, 4-0. Their fans became disgusted and began to pelt the players and umpires with snowballs. It got so bad that the game was stopped, and the Phils won by forfeit.

In another Giant opener, Leon Ames, the New York pitcher, hurled a no-hitter for nine innings, but lost to Brooklyn, 3-0, in the 15th. That same night the Polo Grounds burned to the ground.

There has been a legitimate no-hitter on opening day...Bob Feller of visiting Cleveland did the job against the White Sox in the 1940 opener, winning 1-0.

One of the craziest opening day games came in 1925, when the Cleveland Indians beat the St. Louis Browns, 21-14. The next season saw the Washington Senators and the Philadelphia A's wage a brilliant pitching duel—Walter Johnson bested Ed Rommel, 1-0, in 15 innings.

That was the final opening day appearance for the great Walter Johnson. He bowed out as the top opening day pitcher in history. Starting with the Washington opener in 1910 when he blanked the A's on one hit, he pitched in 14 openers. He won nine of them—and seven of those by shutting out the opposition.

★ ★ ★

In the first American League game played in Detroit —
a year before the league became a "major" league—the Tigers ran into a no-hitter. That was April 19, 1900. And to
add to the general confusion of that opener, the Tigers
kicked in with eight errors. The game was played on the
Tiger Stadium diamond, although the park at that time was
known as Bennett Park. Doc Amole of Buffalo threw the
no-hitter at the Tigers, winning, 8-0. Five Tigers reached
first: two on walks, one on an error, and two were hit by
pitched balls.

In their very next opener, the Tigers did it differently.
There was no no-hitter this time, far from it. That was April
24, 1901, the Tigers' first coming-out party as a "major"
American League city. An overflow crowd of 9,000 turned
out at old Burns Park to see the Tigers battle the Milwaukee
team. Their rivals were led by Hugh Duffy, who had
jumped from the Boston Nationals. He is the same Duffy
who hit .438 with Boston in 1894, which is still the National
League all-time high.

Well, for the first eight innings, most of the Tiger rooters
must have felt the contest to be a dreary one: Milwaukee
led, 13-4, when the Tigers came to bat in the ninth inning.
Then the Detroiters, managed that year by George Stallings,
pulled a rally…and I mean a real rally. The Tigers scored
10 runs and won the game by the score of 14-13—the greatest rally in opening day history. Detroit had 19 hits that afternoon. First baseman Frank Dillon banged out four
doubles. With that feat he still shares a major league record.

★ ★ ★

My last opener as a Tiger broadcaster, in 1993, was a
night game against the A's in California. That event
brought back some great memories.

Several years ago, I met a gentleman and his wife at a party.

"Ernie," the man said, "my wife is an avid fan of WJR and the Tigers. She listens to the station from the early-morning show until bedtime."

"Yes," his wife said. "I even stay up late for those Tiger broadcasts from the West Coast. Many a time during the baseball season I've gone to sleep with Ernie Harwell."

"I'm flattered to hear that," I answered. "But even though you might go to sleep with me, I'm sure you wake up with J.P. McCarthy" (WJR's morning drive-time personality).

Opening the season on the road at night—especially on the West Coast—is not ideal. It's a lot more fun to have that first game at home, in the daytime. I don't remember too many nighttime openers for the Tigers, but one comes immediately to mind. That was at Anaheim in 1967. It was the night Ray Lane made his debut as my partner. Ray was nervous that night, but he did a fine job and went on to be an outstanding partner for seven years.

The first Tigers' opener I broadcast was a road game. The team left Lakeland and went straight to Cleveland to start the 1960 season against the Indians. It was a special game, because at the close of spring training the Tigers had traded American League batting champion Harvey Kuenn (.353) for Cleveland's home run king, Rocky Colavito (42).

Now these two big stars would play against each other, and Cleveland fans were hopping mad about the trade. Rocky was their hero—a sort of matinee idol with muscles.

It was a bitter, cold afternoon. My partner, Hall-of-Famer George Kell, and I worked in a makeshift booth out in the stands. The freezing winds whipped off Lake Erie, and both of us yearned for the end of the game and a chance to thaw out in our hotel room.

Wouldn't you know it? The game lasted 15 innings. For four hours and 54 minutes, the teams battled. Finally, the Tigers won, 4-2. Harvey got the best of Colavito in that first meeting. He doubled and singled. Rock fanned four times and went hitless in six times at bat.

The closeness and excitement of the game warmed us somewhat, but I'll never forget how we shivered that first afternoon together as regular-season Tiger broadcasters.

Weather was a factor on another memorable Tiger opening day in Detroit in 1962. One of my favorite Tigers, Frank Lary, was the pitcher against the Yanks that chilly afternoon. Lary had a bad shoulder, and his spring training had been a poor one. He was having troubles. But that day, the famed "Yankee Killer" Frank Lary, beat the Yanks, 5-3, for the 28th time against only 10 losses. This victory, though, had a tragic cost. Lary pulled up lame running out a triple in the seventh inning. Later, he tried to adjust his pitching motion to favor his leg and hurt his arm. Frank Lary was never the same great pitcher.

Other favorite Tiger openers:

• My first home opener as an announcer at Detroit's Briggs Stadium, 1960. Eighty-degree weather and a packed house. George Kell and I had to redo our pre-game TV interview with Nellie Fox, the White Sox second baseman, three times because of camera and sound problems. I'll never forget how patient and understanding Nellie was that afternoon...

• The Tigers and Toronto Blue Jays sitting idle three days as an April 1982 snowstorm postponed their entire opening series.

• Veteran slugger Darrell Evans making his debut before the Detroit fans with a three-run homer in the 1984 opener...

• Highly touted Chris Pittaro with three hits, sparking the Tigers to victory on opening day, 1985, and then fading quickly to the minors...

Yes, opening day is my favorite baseball day of the year.

12

The Games People Play

"It is also necessary at this season to establish firm emotional connections with a major league ball club, to share the agonies of their defeats and the ecstacies of their triumphs. Without these simple marriages, none of us could survive."—E.B. White

Doubleheaders...they're still with us and have been for a long time. However, there aren't as many in one season as there used to be.

But what about tripleheaders? Has there ever been one? The answer is yes. The last tripleheader was back in 1920. And there were two others—both before the turn of the century. Technically, those two tripleheaders were really not triple-headers, but rather three games played in one day with different admissions.

The tripleheader in 1920 was a pure one...only one admission was charged for three games on October 2. It was the final week of that season. Brooklyn had a big lead in the National League race. The Giants were second and the Reds third. Pittsburgh had an outside chance to pull past the Reds and gain third-place money. But they needed to win all four remaining games, and the Reds needed to lose all of their four.

Then on Friday came the rain. With no make-up dates available, the Pirates had apparently lost their chance. However, Pirate owner Barney Dreyfuss proposed a Saturday tripleheader. Reds manager Pat Moran didn't like the idea. An appeal was made to the league president, John Heydler, and he ruled in favor of the tripleheader.

They did play three games. Cinci won the first two, 13-4 and 7-3. The Pirates won the third, 6-0, when it was called on account of darkness at the end of six innings.

The first game had started at noon. And the three games—or two games and six innings—were played within a span of only five hours. These days, one game often takes three hours, so, by modern standards those 24 innings would have required at least seven or eight hours.

The finish? The teams ended the season in the same order they had been in before Pittsburgh's last-ditch effort: Dodgers, Giants, Reds, and Pirates.

The other so-called tripleheaders happened in the 1890s—both on Labor Days. In 1890, in a Players' League game, host Brooklyn beat Pittsburgh three times, 10-9, 3-2, and 8-4.

Six years later in Baltimore, the Orioles swept the Louisville team three times, 4-3, 9-1, and 12-1. The first game was played in the morning and the other two in the afternoon.

The *Baltimore Sun* told the three-game story in its headlines:
BASEBALL TO BURN.
LOUISVILLE ON THE FIRE IN THREE SUCCESSIVE GAMES.
WARMED UP IN THE FORENOON AND DONE BROWN ON
    BOTH SIDES ON A PRETTY AFTERNOON.

★ ★ ★

The real iron-man show of baseball came in the New England League in 1899. Manchester, with a chance to catch league-leading Portland by winning its last six games, scheduled those six games for the final day of the season.

They began at 9 A.M., playing a doubleheader before lunch, both nine-inning games. Three games were played in the afternoon. At this point, Manchester had won all five. The sixth game was started, but after two innings, Portland protested a decision and walked off the field. So the ump gave Manchester its sixth victory by forfeit. Yet all that work went for nothing. Newport, another contender in the league, won a tripleheader on that last day. Then league officials stepped in and threw out all games except one victory by Newport and one by Manchester. That decision gave the title to Newport. Manchester had played and won six games in one day, and it did the team no good at all.

★ ★ ★

Although the average playing time for a professional baseball game is two-and-a-half hours, the Atlanta and Mobile teams of the Southern League once completed a regulation nine-inning tilt in the record time of 32 minutes.

On September 19, the final day of the 1910 season, Atlanta edged Mobile, 2-1, at Atlanta with one run in the last half of the ninth inning. Batters on both teams waited on very few pitches, most of them swinging at the first offering. The Crackers and the Gulls all ran to and from their positions in changing from offense to defense.

With pitchers Chapelle of Mobile and Griffin of Atlanta showing fine control, only one batter—an Atlantan—drew a base on balls. One Mobile player struck out. And the majority of the batters hit to the infield, as indicated by the 35 assists. Highlighting the game was a fast triple play by the Mobile infield.

Atlanta took the lead with a run in the first on a double, an infield out, and a steal. Mobile tied it on a triple and a wild pitch in the sixth. Then Atlanta triumphed with one tally in the ninth on a single, a stolen base, and another single.

On the same afternoon at Nashville, Tennessee, Nashville and New Orleans completed a game in 42 minutes. They thought they had set a new mark until they read the sports pages the following morning.

In the opposite direction, the longest game on record is one played at Carrolton, Kentucky, during the 1868 season. It started at 10 A.M. and lasted until it was called on account of darkness at 6 P.M. At that time, only seven innings had been completed.

★ ★ ★

There's always been a fascination about no-hitters, and one of the most fascinating was one in which the Tigers participated. What makes it fascinating? The fact that the Tigers were victims of no-hit pitching, but still managed to win the game.

The Orioles had broken an 0-0 tie in the eighth inning. With the bases loaded and one out, Luis Aparicio hit a fly to right. Al Kaline caught it, but his throw to Bill Freehan was wild and Curt Blefary scored on the sacrifice.

So the lefthander Steve Barber took a 1-0 lead and a no-hitter into the ninth. Norm Cash led off the Tiger ninth with a walk. Ray Oyler also walked. Dick Tracewski came in to run for Cash. He and Oyler advanced on pitcher Earl Wilson's sacrifice bunt.

Willie Horton then pinch-hit and fouled out. Barber needed only one more out for his no-hitter. Jake Wood came in to run for Oyler. Then Barber threw a curve into the dirt. The pitch got past catcher Larry Haney, and Tracewski raced home to tie the game, 1-1. Wood moved to third on the same wild pitch. Barber then walked Mickey Stanley.

Oriole manager Hank Bauer made a pitching change. No-hitter or not, that was all for Barber. Yes, he had a no-hitter, but he had walked 10 and hit two batters. Stu Miller took over to try to get the final out—third baseman Don

Wert. Wert hit a grounder to Aparicio, and the shortstop tossed the ball to Mark Belanger for what would have been the final out. But Belanger dropped the ball. Wood came home with the winning run. Miller preserved the no-hitter by getting Kaline on a force. But the Tigers now had the lead.

Fred Gladding replaced Earl Wilson on the mound for the Tigers in the bottom of the ninth. He got Frank and Brooks Robinson and Mike Epstein in order to end the game and give the Tigers the victory, 2-1.

★ ★ ★

When the Tigers smashed their way to two 20-run games in the first week of their 1993 home season, they were the talk of the baseball neighborhood.

Forty years ago, they were in two similar games at Fenway Park—when they were the bashed instead of the bashers. On June 17, 1953, the Red Sox killed the Tigers, 17-1. Boston collected 20 hits off four Tiger pitchers. The only Detroit run came in the ninth and was unearned.

The next afternoon, Boston beat the Tigers, 23-3. The Red Sox scored 17 runs in the seventh inning. Detroit manager Fred Hutchinson, known for his terrible temper, told off his players after the fiasco. "It was the worst demonstration I ever saw—worse than any high school team," he said.

The 17-run inning is a modern major league record. Gene Stephens banged out three hits in that inning, also a record. Boston's 14-hit total remains a modern major league record for one inning; 17 is still the most RBIs in any inning, and the 11 singles is the American League record for the most in one frame.

Those were some of the Boston feats that humiliated the Tigers in that fateful seventh inning at Fenway. Three Tigers pitchers tried to stop the onslaught—Steve Gromek, Dick Weik, and Earl Harris. The game marked Gromek's Tiger debut; three days earlier, Detroit traded Owen Friend, Art Houtteman, Bill Wight, and Joe Ginsberg to Cleveland for pitchers Gromek, Weik, Al Aber, and infielder Ray Boone.

Gromek must have wondered about the team he was joining. His first look at the Tigers as a team member had been the 17-1 game, which he watched in silence from the bullpen. Then he pitched the next day in that 17-run Boston inning and was charged with nine runs.

When Hutchinson pulled him from the game, Gromek's first thought was that he was through after just one performance. But all Fred said was: "Steve, you'll start when we get to Philadelphia."

He did start—and blanked the A's on four hits for his first victory as a Tiger.

But the '53 season was not a good one for our heroes. They finished sixth and were 40½ games out of first place—but made the recordbook with that one horrendous inning in Boston. And they put the Red Sox there, too.

★ ★ ★

I got a question not too long ago from an avid baseball fan in Chillicothe, Ohio—Len Sabatini. Len asked what my most disappointing Tiger losses were.

Mr. Sabatini suggested the Tiger-Yankee game of September 1, 1961. Certainly, that's near the top of my list. The Tigers went into Yankee Stadium that Labor-Day weekend only one-and-a-half games behind the league-leading Yankees. The Detroit Lions had a pre-season football game scheduled in Detroit that same night. They postponed it because of the great interest in the Tiger pennant chase and because of the fact that we'd be on TV that evening with the Tiger-Yankee game.

Unfortunately, the Yankees won that one, 1-0. They won it on a single in the ninth by Moose Skowron. The Yanks' Whitey Ford and the Tigers' Don Mossi had dueled away until the Moose got that winning hit. From then on, it was downhill for the Tigers. The Yankees swept the series and before a week had passed, the Tigers had dropped to 10 games back. The race was over.

That Yankees team was one of the greatest in baseball history, winning 109 games. The Tigers, finishing second, won 101. The Yankees' Roger Maris hit his record 61 home runs and Mickey Mantle hit 54. The Tigers' Norm Cash won the league batting crown with a .361 average and Al Kaline was second with .324. Quite a year for the two old rivals.

Four American League teams have finished second and won 100 games or more: the Tigers of 1915 and 1961, the Orioles of 1980, and the Yankees of 1954. The 1954 Yankees won 103 games in a 154-game schedule and still finished behind the Cleveland Indians. The Indians won 111 that year.

Another disappointing Tiger loss came on the final day of the 1967 season. The California Angels beat Detroit, 8-5, in the second game of a doubleheader to knock them out of the pennant race. Then there was that devastating defeat—again at the hands of the Angels—on August 29, 1986. The Tigers led, 12-5, going into the last of the ninth. The Angels rallied, topping off the comeback with a Dick Schofield grand-slam home run to beat Detroit, 13-12.

All of those losses left a bad taste in my mouth. But I think the most disappointing Tiger defeat in my 34 years of broadcasting their games came in the World Series of 1968. It was a gloomy, rainy Sunday, October 6, the fourth game of the Series. The Tigers were down, two games to one, and were playing badly. And on that rainy Sunday in Detroit they were worse than ever. Some of my friends were honoring me with a party downtown that night. Many of the writers and other media people were coming. But the game dragged on. It was interrupted several times by heavy showers. Any other time it would have been postponed, but not this time—this was the World Series. The

Tigers were behind, 6-0, in the fifth inning. Many of the fans left, and the game still dragged on.

I got a sinking feeling that my party would be a bust. All the writers would be working into the night; the other media people would be wet, tired, and disgusted and wouldn't want to show up.

It was one of the worst-played games I have ever seen—and this was a World Series. The game finally ended with the Cards beating Detroit, 10-1.

Strangely enough, the party came off in great fashion. The folks did show up, and we had a great time. But the game lives in my memory as one of the worst and most disappointing in my 34 years with the Tigers.

★ ★ ★

During my 34 years of Tigers broadcasting, I was often asked to name an all-time Tiger team. Well, here it is. My selections will be restricted to those players I've seen in action from 1960 through the 1993 season. You'll likely disagree with my picks, and that's what makes it fun.

My first baseman is Norman Cash. He was a batting champion with home run power. I'll pick another first baseman, Cecil Fielder, who hits the ball harder and farther than anybody I've ever seen.

Second base belongs to Lou Whitaker. Steadiness and longevity put him on my team. Lou is underrated as a hitter. In the clutch or with two strikes on him, he is one of the best.

I have no doubts about shortstop. It has to be Alan Trammell. Tram does everything well. He led the team in batting in 1993 for the seventh time in the last 14 years. His shortstop play is as consistent as anyone's.

At third, I debated but decided to take Aurelio Rodriguez over Don Wert. Both were good. But Rodriguez had a better arm—a true rifle—and was a better hitter than Don. I always felt that Aurelio, with his great arm, should have switched to pitching.

My outfield would consist of Al Kaline, Willie Horton, and Rocky Colavito. Kaline, the Hall-of-Famer, was the consummate professional. He was a consistent hitter who often could supply the home run. Nobody in my American League time ever played right field any better than Al. Horton was less talented in the field but was a powerful clutch hitter. He contributed many a clutch Tiger RBI. And don't knock the Rock. Colavito was one of the Tigers' most colorful stars. His home run power was awesome, and he had an outstanding arm.

I'll take two catchers, Bill Freehan and Lance Parrish. Bill lasted longer and was probably better on defense. He also was a great leader. Parrish could throw well and gave the Tigers consistent long-ball power.

Because it's my team and I can do what I want, I am going to pick three starting pitchers and three relievers. My right-handers are Denny McLain and Jack Morris. Denny was sensational in 1968 with 32 victories, including one in the World Series. He followed the next year with 24. And he had earlier posted a 20-victory year in 1966.

Jack Morris lasted longer with the Tigers and through the years was a more dominant pitcher. He was the team's ultimate stopper.

My lefthander is Mickey Lolich, 1968 World Series hero with three victories over the Cardinals. Mickey was a true workhorse. He pitched more than 300 innings in four straight seasons, and in 1971 and '72 won 25 and 22, respectively.

For my bull pen, I pick Mike Henneman, who holds the all-time Tigers save record; John Hiller, the left-handed ace in the 1960s and '70s; and Willie Hernandez, who helped the Tigers to a Series title with his 32 saves in 1984.

For my pinch-hitter, my choice is Gates Brown. He handled the toughest job in baseball in great style and is certainly the best Tiger I ever saw in that role.

That's my team.

★ ★ ★

As in all history, baseball history often creates myths about teams and stars. In time, the margin between myth and truth seems to dim. Finally, we have difficulty separating the truth from the legend.

There are many myths about the Yankees, whose 1927 team is considered by most baseball experts to be the greatest in history:

1. *The 1927 Yankees were the first to be called "Murderers' Row."*

Wrong! The term "Murderers' Row" was given to the Yankees in 1919 by Robert Ripley. Even before he started his "Believe It or Not" cartoon, Ripley drew a sports cartoon of Frank Baker, Roger Peckinpaugh, Wally Pipp, and Del Pratt and dubbed them "Murderers' Row."

2. *Yankees owner Jacob Ruppert put his players in pinstripe uniforms to fashion a slimmer look for the overweight Babe Ruth.*

Wrong! The New Yorkers first wore pinstripes April 22, 1915, five years before Ruth joined them.

3. *Babe Ruth called his famous 1932 World Series home run off pitcher Charlie Root.*

Wrong! Doubtful testimony dims the truth. In overkill, it is baseball's answer to the unending investigation of the John F. Kennedy assassination.

4. *The 1927 Yankees had baseball's best-ever record at 110-44.*

Wrong! They don't even hold the American League record. That belongs to the Cleveland Indians of 1954, who won 111 and lost 43. The major league record was set by the 1906 Chicago Cubs. They won 116 and lost 36.

5. *When Babe Ruth hit 60 home runs in 1927, several of his homers bounced into the stands.*

Wrong! It is true that a bounce-in drive was a home run in 1927, but careful research has revealed that all of Ruth's 60 homers reached the seats or beyond on the fly.

6. *Babe Ruth hit three home runs at Pittsburgh in the final three times at bat in his career.*
Wrong! These homers were the Babe's last hurrah. But he played several games after that and retired five days after his Pittsburgh performance.
7. *The 1927 Yankees team drew tremendous crowds.*
Wrong! Earlier Yankees teams in 1920 and 1921 outdrew the '27 team. The best drawing team in Yankees history was the 1988 club, which attracted 2,633,701. The 1927 Yankees drew 1,164,015.
8. *Lou Gehrig's streak of 2,130 straight regular-season games—out of the 2,164 in his career—began when he replaced Wally Pipp at first base after Pipp's famous headache.*
Wrong! Gehrig had started his streak the day before, June 1, 1925, with a pinch-hit performance. Also, he had appeared in 23 games for New York spanning 1923-24.

★ ★ ★

They were the greatest—that Yankee team of 1927: Babe Ruth, Lou Gehrig, Earle Combs, Herb Pennock, Tony Lazzeri, and Waite Hoyt. Baseball history has forever deemed that aggregation the outstanding baseball team of all time...and those names are enshrined in the Hall of Fame at Cooperstown.

But what about some of the others on that team? What about these names: Julie Wera, Joe Giard, Mike Gazella, Ray Morehart, John Grabowski, and Pat Collins? Not only have they missed the Hall of Fame, they're not even household names—except probably in their own households. All of which only proves that even the great teams are filled with players who are easily forgotten, and now exist only as a footnote in the agate type of baseball history.

We all remember the greats and forget the little guys. But the little guys have their roles, too. On a baseball team that role is sometimes that of a talented utility man, or a pinch-hitter, or maybe a player who is just a holler-guy—the kind who keeps spirits up on a team.

For instance, on that great Yankee team of '27, Julie Wera was a third baseman who played 38 games and batted .238. Ray Morehart was a reserve second baseman. In 73 games, he batted .256, hit one home run, and knocked in 20 runs. Those Yanks had three catchers—none really outstanding with the bat. Pat Collins was the No. 1 receiver. He was 30 years old and batted .275, in a year when it was almost a disgrace to be under the .300 mark. The other catchers were John Grabowski, who hit .277, and Benny Bengough, who batted only .247. Neither of these two had a home run, and Collins hit only seven. The great Bill Dickey was to break into the lineup the following season.

Other "filler-inners" were Mike Gazella, the little infielder, who hit .278, and outfielder Cedric Durst, who batted .248, but didn't have a home run all season.

The Yankee pitching staff of '27 had one 20-game winner. He was Waite Hoyt, who pulled in 22 victories. Wilcy Moore (19), Herb Pennock (19), and Urban Shocker (18) were the other pitching stars.

But that staff had its "hangers-on" too: Myles Thomas, who won only seven, and Joe Giard, who appeared in 16 games, didn't win one and had an earned-run average of eight.

Not everybody is a star. It takes the little-known guys, too, even on a team as great the New York Yankees of 1927.

★ ★ ★

What was the toughest, most dedicated team in baseball history? I think a lot of sportswriters would agree on one—the Baltimore Orioles of the 1890s. Here was a team that invented all types of new strategy and fought and scrapped its way to championships. Aching muscles and injuries never stopped them. They were so immune to hurt that they contributed a well-known expression to the lore of the game: "Take it like an Old Oriole."

Well, Hughie Jennings was an Old Oriole—one of the most famous. Like the others, he was tough, and he'd get on base any way he could—regardless of physical safety. One afternoon in a close game, Jennings let himself be hit in the head by a pitch.

As Hughie trotted to first base holding his injured noggin, a Baltimore bleacherite yelled to him: "Thata boy, Hughie. That's putting the wood to it."

13

Strange, But (Mostly) True

"Baseball is a game where a curve is an optical illusion, a screw-ball can be a pitch or a person, stealing is legal and you can spit anywhere you like except in the umpire's eye or on the ball."
—Jim Murray

Baseball is a great game—our favorite pastime. But you must admit it is sometimes goofy. Take a look at presidents of the two major leagues. The National League president was (Bill) White. White is black. The American League president is (Bobby) Brown. Brown is white.

Baseball is one of the few businesses in which competitors are also partners. No wonder the owners make so many illogical decisions.

In baseball's literature, we celebrate the ultimate symbol of failure (the Mighty Casey striking out) and focus an inordinate amount of attention on confusion (trying to determine Who's on First).

The first rule in the baseball rule book says, "Baseball is a game played between two teams of nine players each." Yet in the American League (and in most minor leagues) each team has 10 players.

Rain checks are issued for indoor stadiums. Umpires ruin new balls before each game by rubbing them with mud from the Delaware River.

Old men wear knickers, and young men grow beards. The highest-paid performer in the minor leagues is a mascot called the Chicken. In the major leagues the hirelings make more money than their bosses.

A batted ball that hits the foul line is called fair. The word strike (which means to hit an object) is used when a batter misses a pitch or doesn't even swing at it.

In what other sport does a dog own a world championship ring?

In baseball, spring training begins in the winter, and the World Series is confined to North America.

The left-hand batter's box is on the same side of the field as right field. Over the door of the visitors' clubhouse the sign says: No Visitors.

Finally, if baseball is such a great family game, why don't we honor Pop Fly as the Father of Baseball?

I tell you, baseball is a goofy game.

★ ★ ★

Some facts and thoughts about the baseball scene:

Umpires never say "play ball" or "batter up"...only in books and in the movies. . . . The baseball rule book does not give us a definition which distinguishes a mitt from a glove...Most pitching coaches and managers feel that using the split-finger pitch is detrimental to the pitcher's arm.

Why do we baseball people say "flied out" instead of "flew out"? Why is home plate so-called instead of being fourth base? When a pitch is not a strike, why do we call it a ball? Wouldn't some other term better fit the situation?

Isn't "road trip" redundant? Or can you take a "home trip"? A so-called ground-rule double is not a part of the ground rules but is from the rule book itself...Theoretically, a team can't rally unless it comes from behind; but the word is often used in stories and broadcasts when a team does some heavy scoring, regardless of the game situation.

Nominations for overrated: Trade rumors, saves, ERA, clubhouse quotes, exclusive stories, outdoor eating at cafes, the Olympics, baseball giveaways, college football ratings, and the changeup.

Underrated: The hit-and-run, the bunt, sportsmanship, cornbread, radio newscasts, pajamas, baseball umpires, official scorers, live music at the ballpark, TV directors of sports events, newspaper copy editors, and pitchers' windups.

I am amazed at the number of avid baseball fans who've never seen a minor league game. I was very lucky to broadcast in the minors for three years. It was certainly a learning experience. As a fan, I grew up with the Atlanta Crackers in the old Southern League. They were my boyhood heroes.

Certainly, being part of minor league baseball gives you a true appreciation of the majors. I've always admired the players who love the game so much that they stick around and play minor league baseball. They know they'll never make it to the big leagues; but they simply don't want to give up because they love the game.

Many years ago, a player could do almost as well financially in some of the higher minors as he could in the big leagues. But those days are gone forever. He plays in the minors for two reasons now: 1.) Because he loves to play, or 2.) To serve an apprenticeship with the hope that someday he will make it to the big leagues.

Strangely enough, there are some players who have hit better in the major leagues than in the minors. Reason: The lights are better, and pitchers aren't as wild in the big leagues.

Everybody says, "I'll be ready when the bell rings." But who rings the bell? And what about that "green light" the batters are always getting.

The language of the game must be confusing to someone who didn't grow up with it.

★ ★ ★

Here are some questions I thought you'd never ask:
*Why do the managers and coaches in baseball wear uniforms
when those in other sports wear street clothes?*
The manager of baseball's first pro team was Harry
Wright, a center fielder. Naturally, he had to wear a uni-
form. And baseball managers have worn uniforms ever
since...
When did battery signs originate?
They were first used by Connie Mack when he was
catching for Washington in 1888...
What team sponsored the first bat day?
The St. Louis Browns. In 1952 their business manager,
Rudy Schaffer, bought 12,000 bats at a close-out sale and
gave them away at a doubleheader. The Browns drew
15,000 for that first bat day...
*What event prompted the retirement of Leo Durocher the
player?*
When the slow-footed Ernie Lombardi hit a grounder
to Leo and beat it out, Leo knew he was through. It was
1945 and Durocher was 40 years old and had played for 17
years in the major leagues...
What was Bob Uecker's advice for catching a knuckle ball?
Wait till the ball stops rolling, then pick it up...
What was the quietest game in baseball history?
A game between the New York Giants and Jersey City
in Jersey City on Sunday, April 19, 1919. Sunday baseball
was illegal in Jersey City, so the officials insisted that the
fans refrain from noisemaking. The game was completely
devoid of cheering, booing, or any other kind of noise...
*What manager would not allow his team to use the visitors'
clubhouse in an away World Series game?*

John McGraw. McGraw hated the New York Yankees so much that he kicked them out of his ballpark, the Polo Grounds. When the Giants played the Yanks in the 1923 World Series, McGraw refused to let his team use the clubhouse at Yankee Stadium...

To what player did the expression, "Good field, no hit" first apply?

Mike Gonzales, scouting for the Cardinals, put that label on Moe Berg, who later became a major leaguer and a World War II spy...

★ ★ ★

Here are a few questions I ask *myself* about baseball:

How can personal relationships on a baseball team differ so much in summer and winter?

For seven months players on a team are very close. They live in the same hotels, ride the same team bus and plane, dress and undress in the same clubhouse. Their goals are the same. Their successes and failures are all shared with each other.

The camaraderie on a major league team is like that of a Marine platoon or a college fraternity. Inside jokes prevail. There is always good-natured banter, and sometimes frayed feelings from overheated tempers.

Indeed a baseball team is one big (and not always so happy) family. Some players room together on the road. This custom is fading, but there are still a few players who like to share a room. Such a situation would epitomize the closeness of the players to each other.

"Come on, roomie," one says. "Let's go eat." And they go out together to their favorite restaurant. Or maybe to a movie. Or maybe they just sit and talk for hours.

But once the off-season comes and they go to their separate winter homes, that closeness is gone. I've talked to many of them and have found that very few continue to be in contact over the winter months. Out of sight, out of mind.

The same situation holds when playing days are over. Players who played and lived together for one team over a period of 10 to 15 years, leave the game and seldom come into contact with each other again. They have their own interests, and they go their own way.

In the summer of 1984, Glenn Abbott pitched for the Detroit Tigers. A marginal performer, he was farmed to Evansville and brought back. Later in mid-season he was released and returned to his home in Arkansas. Glenn was one of the most popular Tigers, and his teammates sincerely regretted seeing him go.

Yet, when I tried to get his phone number from even his closest friends, not one of them had it. None had been in contact with him after his release. Finally, Doug Bair, a fellow Tiger pitcher, came up with Glenn's address. But the point is: Once he left the scene, not a single Tiger had been in contact with this team favorite.

Why do players suffer with tunnel vision concerning their profession?

The average big leaguer knows and cares almost nothing about the history of baseball. Even current statistics find him only mildly interested—except for his own batting average or ERA. Some players know the ins and outs of the pension plan and understand the regulations of the Players' Association. Yet, most care little about the lore, legend, or history of the game that provides them a livelihood.

I can cite two notable exceptions: Pete Rose and Reggie Jackson. Pete not only knew up-to-date exactly how many hits, doubles, triples, etc., he had, but he also knew where he stood on the all-time lists. He could locate his place in any baseball historical category.

Reggie Jackson had that same quality. Reggie, of all the players I've known, seemed to sense a feeling of baseball history. He admired and appreciated the stars of the past—

even without reference to his own place in a historical framework.

Some players have evinced an interest in the game apart from their own roles because of their off-the-diamond professions. For example, Buck Martinez did an excellent job as a player-commentator during the regular baseball season and also served on the Canadian network for play-off and World Series broadcasts. Others have written columns for the daily papers during their playing careers. And, there have been many who went into post-career jobs of announcing and writing.

But the player who plays and does little else is, on average, almost oblivious to what is happening around him. Joe Falls, the *Detroit News* columnist, has been writing sports since the late 1940s. Joe told me that in all his career, only one player has ever asked him about his job — what he does, how he goes about it, and other details.

As a broadcaster for more than 40 years, I had few players ever mention that they had heard me on the air. I'm sure some did and just didn't think to say so. But many baseball executives, scouts, umpires, and others from all other facets of the game constantly told me they had heard broadcasts. The players? Very few.

Baseball is the most tradition-bound and highly structured of all sports. Why then is there no order in the location of the dugouts?

In the various parks, some home dugouts are near third base; some are on the first-base side of the field.

In 1955, Baltimore Oriole manager Paul Richards changed the home dugout from the first- to third-base side. He did it for two reasons: The sun shone into the first-base dugout in the late afternoon, beating down with intense heat and blinding the view from the dugout; and behind the third-base dugout was the Oriole office. Richards was wheeling and dealing that season as both manager and general manager of the Orioles.

I know of no other situation in which a team picked a dugout location for a particular reason.

Why do different sports have different names for the clubhouse?

In baseball, it's a clubhouse. Football players dress in a locker room. Both basketball and hockey players use a dressing room.

In the old days of baseball some of the teams actually dressed in a house behind the stands. Crosley Field in Cincinnati provided that kind of facility. Also, baseball teams are still called clubs. So, it's not illogical that the players should use the term "clubhouse."

The football locker room comes from early gym days. Also, the various athletic departments always maintained lockers for the collegiate athletes.

I believe the dressing room terminology is derived from the fact that basketball and hockey professional games are played in auditoriums or arenas that also produce various shows and exhibitions.

What do players carry in those briefcases?

On every plane trip with a baseball team you see almost every player carrying a briefcase. Seldom do I see one of the cases opened on the plane.

Now, a player's bag is presumably packed with his personal clothing, toilet kit, and the usual items with which a traveler travels. His uniform, spikes, and other equipment go with the team equipment. So what does he have to put into a briefcase?

Richie Hebner, the ex-gravedigger, used to stow away whiskey miniatures in his briefcase when he was with the Tigers. And in the summer of the great Tiger season of 1984, I saw Aurelio Lopez' briefcase pop open as he boarded the team bus in Kansas City airport. What popped out of Señor Smoke's case? Was it a smoke bomb? No, it was a tiny bottle of Tabasco.

These two items are the only ones I've ever seen from a

ballplayer's briefcase. Maybe they carry paperback books, or the *Wall Street Journal*, or letters from their lawyers and agents. Perhaps a cassette player and tapes. Until someone opens a briefcase and inspects it, we'll just have to keep wondering.

★ ★ ★

Complaints! Complaints! Complaints! Why is everybody always complaining? Why am I complaining about everybody complaining? Doesn't it seem that complaining—not baseball—just might be our national pastime?

Baseball certainly has its complaints. They come from fans, and from people in the game. And these complaints, for the most part, are directed toward the owner, the general manager, the manager, the groundskeeper, the writer, and the broadcaster.

These are the most common complaints aimed at these people and others:

To the owner: You're making too many changes. You're bound too much by tradition. You should spend more for good players. You are paying your players too much. You interfere in the running of the team. You don't take enough interest in the team.

To the general manager: I can never get a good ticket to the game. All the seats have been taken. You are always making bad player deals.

To the manager: You don't have your team bunt enough. You take your pitchers out too quickly. You leave your pitchers in the game too long.

To the third base coach: You're too aggressive. You send runners home, and they are always thrown out at the plate. You're too timid. You hold up runners, and they never score.

To the player: You don't hustle enough. You make too

much money. Why don't you sign autographs? You should speak at our banquet. We'll even give you a free meal!
   To the umpire: You always favor the other team. Our team never seems to get any close calls from you. Why can't you hurry up the game? They take too long. You are too quick to toss a player out of the game. You should bear down on the players and control them better.
   To the concessions manager: The prices are too high. The hot dogs are cold. Your beer is not strong enough. The lines are too long.
   To the groundskeeper: The infield is too hard. Grounders get through too easily. The infield is too soft. We can't turn the double play. Why can't you fix the mound right?
   To the broadcaster: You repeat too much. You don't give the score often enough. You're a homer. Why don't you root for the home team more? You're too critical of the players. You're not objective enough, and you never seem to be critical of the players. The commercials are too long.
   To the writer: You're too nosy, always prying into the players' private lives. You write too much detail. Give us more of the human side of the players. You never write positive articles about the hometeam.
   Everybody leads the league in complaints. They are simply part of baseball—just as they are part of the outside world.

★ ★ ★

When you've been around baseball for a while you see all sorts of players. They come in different shapes, sizes, and temperaments. Most of them fit into one of these categories:
   1. *Billy the Bandage:* An adhesive-tape worm. Keeps himself on pills and needles…First in the whirlpool, first on the rubbing table, last on the field (a rub-tub-sub)…He has tried every medicine. Next week, embalming fluid…Even the look he gives you is a hurt look. Not only are his ail-

ments chronic, they're chronicles...Always in the punk of condition.

2. *Lover Louis:* Never married, but he has had a lot of near Mrs...Troubled by curves...More effective at night— late at night. Will chase anything but a flyball.

3. *Belligerent Basil:* One half of a fight looking for the other half. He'd climb a mountain to take a punch at an echo...Loves a fight so much, he has been married six times.

4. *Porous Paul:* He couldn't stop a grapefruit from rolling uphill. Plays every hop perfectly—except the last one...No matter where his manager puts him in the lineup, he can't hide him from the opposition. Leads league in runs-booted-in....A holier-than-thou defensive debit.

5. *Orville and Out:* The pitcher's best friend. As a hitter, he has ruined more rallies than tear gas...Qualifies for a trapeze act because his only attributes are a swing and a miss.

6. *Slow Freight Freddie:* It takes a triple to score him from third...He not only runs like he has a piano on his back, he also stops and plays "God Bless America" on the way...Nickname is *E Pluribus Unum* because he can't get off a dime.

7. *Percentage Patrick:* His mother must have been frightened by a computer because he is forever figuring... Can't remember whether his team won or lost, but he can tell you his batting average to the final percentage point...Officious with the official scorer.

8. *Conceited Charles:* In love with himself—and he has no competition...A case of mistaken nonentity...Suffers from I strain...On his 24th birthday he sent a telegram of congratulations to his mother...Hasn't an enemy in the world, but all his friends hate him.

9. *Stuffer Sam:* If calories counted in the official averages, he would be leading the league...Way out in front. Always exceeding the feed limit...Far from his old sylph... Sure to get his just desserts.

10. Raver Ralph: Named year after year as the game's Most Voluble Player...A man who pops off even more than he pops up. Often is thrown out spieling...Mama's little yelper...Approaches every subject with an open mouth. His future is in the radio or TV booth.

11. Money Man Marvin: Only sign he doesn't miss is the dollar sign. Spends more time with his agent than with his teammates...Doesn't care if the game is on the line—only if his signature is...Rather see a pitch from his broker than from a hard-throwing opponent.

★ ★ ★

There's no sustained thrill in sports that can match a close baseball pennant race. Here are 25 things bound to happen as we head down the stretch:

• The managers of the contending clubs will say, "It all depends on pitching."
• Television camera crews will go on the road with the team.
• Each TV station will feature interviews with loud fans in loud bars.
• A rookie reliever will pick up a surprise victory.
• A non-contender will use an unknown pitcher against a contender. The other contenders will protest; yet the unknown probably will win.
• Radio stations will be flooded with new songs about the team.
• The newspaper will send three more staffers to each game.
• Each paper will issue a special section with profiles of the players
• Ads to buy and sell tickets will appear in the classifieds.
• More players will do TV and radio commercials.
• The teams' front offices will say: "We're making every effort to strengthen the team, but we're not going to wreck our farm system."

- A key player will suffer a severe injury and miss the rest of the season.
- Sudden rains will create unwanted doubleheaders.
- A player will say, "This is what baseball is all about."
- Another will say, "Now it's fun to come to the ballpark."
- Bumper stickers saluting the team will spring up all over the city.
- Some fans will be surprised when the ballpark is not sold out for every game down the stretch.
- Disgruntled millionaire players won't understand why the club can't renegotiate their contracts in the final three weeks.
- The magic number suddenly emerges.
- All the Dopesters become Iffy, and everybody tries to figure which team has the schedule advantage.
- The team wins three straight, and one of the coaches refuses to change his underwear.
- Although losing a game, a team will clinch the division and will be accused of backing in.
- Another team will be accused of choking when it loses two in a row.
- One team will be favored because "it's been through this kind of pressure before."
- Underdog players will say, "We're as good as those high-talented guys because we put our pants on one leg at a time."

★ ★ ★

Dashing through some dots and dotting all the dashes...
Day baseball is coming back and I welcome it. Many clubs have discovered a market for the afternoon game. At one time the players had a rule that all getaway games had to be played in the afternoon. Over the years the rule vanished. Now, many of the big leaguers would like to see the rule reinstated...

In a twisted sort of way, I miss the Yankees' domination of the American League. When the Yanks were supreme, everybody hated them, and they were a terrific drawing card wherever they played. Now, though they're improving, they're just another team. Equity has set in, and the Yankees don't dominate the standings or the attendance figures anymore...

I don't buy the theory that the Texas heat keeps the Rangers from a decent second half of a season. St. Louis and Cincinnati are hot towns and they've had plenty of champions. And what about the great minor league teams that played in Dallas and Fort Worth? Heat didn't seem to stop them in the pennant drives...

Speaking of heat, I believe that air conditioning has made all of us more conscious of it. We go from a cool home, auto, or office, and the heat hits us much harder than it did in the old days when we didn't know anything about air conditioning. Also, don't you think air conditioning is one of the culprits in the increase in sore arms among ballplayers? In the broadcasting business, I'm used to heat. There's always an abundance of hot air in our broadcast booth...

Here's one for you folks who crave trivia: I wonder, when Kansas City Royals' pitcher Billy Brewer beat Milwaukee, whether it was the first time a pitcher ever defeated a major league club with the same last name?...

How is this for far-out? There is now a proposal for the inclusion of a "dirt save" in the official records. Its definition is a statistic "credited to a catcher when he deflects a legally pitched ball that goes in the dirt which, in the official scorer's judgment, prohibited any and all base runners from advancing..."

Over the years, I've built up a collection of baseball scoring rules that I think are questionable, at best. Here are two of my favorites:

Pet peeve No. 1: Giving an assist to a fielder when a batter or runner is not retired. Rule 10.11 says: "An assist shall be credited to each fielder who throws or deflects a batted or thrown ball in such a way that a putout results, or would have resulted except for a subsequent error by any fielder."

Let's take an example. The batter hits a grounder to the second baseman. He throws to first, and the first baseman drops the ball for an error. The batter is safe. Yet the second baseman gets an assist.

Why an assist? What did he assist in doing? The batter was safe, not out.

In football, if a quarterback's pass is dropped by an end, the quarterback is not credited with a completion. If a basketball player passes to a teammate who misses a layup, he doesn't get an assist. In baseball it has always been backward, and I don't understand it.

Pet peeve No. 2: Rule 10.08 says: "A runner shall be charged as 'caught stealing' if he is put out, or would have been put out by an errorless play when he tries to steal."

Example: Runner on first breaks for second. Catcher throws the ball to the shortstop, who drops the ball. The runner is charged "caught stealing."

Does that make sense? Of course not. How can a runner be caught stealing when he is safe? It would be just as logical to say a batter would have hit a home run if the outfielder hadn't caught the ball. I don't get it. The man is standing on second, but the recordbook says he is caught stealing.

★ ★ ★

Major league baseball uniforms get more colorful each year; but they'll probably never reach the rainbow peak they achieved in one of the early seasons of professional ball—1882.

That year the National League adopted a rule that required a different colored uniform for each position. The officials adopted the regulation to add a little gaiety to the game and also to help the fans identify the players, since numbers were not used.

The rule provided that each player be outfitted with a shirt and cap of a certain color to indicate his position: pitcher, light blue; catcher, scarlet; first baseman, scarlet and white; second baseman, orange and black; shortstop, maroon; third baseman, gray and white; left fielder, white; center fielder, red and black; and right fielder, gray. Utility players wore green and brown.

The teams tried the rule for one year and then gave it up.

★ ★ ★

The diamond ring symbolized romance to modern Americans, but the baseball diamond at one time was the most influential factor in the courtship of young Filipinos.

When soon-to-be President William Howard Taft was governor of the Philippines in the early 1900s, he was dismayed by the prevalence of head-hunting among some of the natives. So, with the help of soldiers, sailors, and marines serving in the islands, he introduced baseball to the aborigines hoping it would sublimate their savagery.

Tribes in the mountain sections of the Philippines maintained an ancient custom that before a young Filipino could marry the girl of his choice, he must hang on the wall of his hut the scalp of his most bitter enemy. However, once the athletes learned the finer points of baseball, they changed their custom to one of sportsmanship.

Under the new diamond tradition, it was decreed that before the young suitor could marry his "best," he must hit a home run. Native "Ladies' Days" attracted the belles to the contests to see their beaux—performing in uniforms consisting solely of a healthy smile and a loin cloth.

Americans, acting as muscle-bound cupids, often played simple grounders and easy outs into home runs so their Filipino friends could escape bachelorhood.

But the ones who profited most by the switch in tradition were the suitors' enemies. Under the new custom, they managed to keep their heads while yelling, "Kill the umpire."

★ ★ ★

Many big league baseball players don't want to admit it, but fear often has its turn at bat in the major leagues. It takes many forms. Some players fear failure, some fear success. And some fear being hit by a pitched ball.

Several years ago one successful major league catcher had to fight fear when he came to bat. His manager ordered the catcher to signal to his pitcher for a brush-back pitch.

"Skip," he told his manager. "I don't like to do that. The other pitcher knows where that brush-back sign came from, and he'll retaliate when I'm at the plate."

Careers have been ruined by the fear of being hit. Many minor leaguers don't make it to the majors because they can't subdue their fear. Major leaguers lose their skills after beanball incidents.

"Don Wert was never the same hitter after he had been hit by a pitch," says Gates Brown, who was Wert's Tiger teammate.

Others can conquer or subdue the fear.

"The best I ever saw at that," Gates says, "was Willie Horton. He got hit on the bill of the helmet. His eye was swollen shut. He came back and crowded the plate even more."

In his first full year with the Tigers, 1964, Gates received a beanball baptism.

"It was the most scared I've ever been," he says. "Pedro Ramos was pitching against us in Cleveland. Kaline had hit two shots off him. I stepped into the box. He wasn't even looking at the plate when he cut one loose at my head. It was the only time I ever heard the umpire yell, 'Look out!'"

Gates points out that the hitter must try to put the brush-back out of his mind. If not, he loses his concentration and is an easy victim for the pitcher.

Ask Dave Winfield, the Twins' slugger, about fear, and he says: "I don't think it's fear. With me it's an uncertainty. When I don't succeed, that uncertainty builds in me. But I have to be aggressive and have no fear of being hit. I can't be intimidated by the pitcher. Often the pitchers feel that they have to pitch me inside. If I think it is intentional, I'll go out toward the mound and tell 'em about it."

Winfield points to Don Baylor as a hitter who couldn't be intimidated. "He was right on top of the plate. They'd pitch him in tight. He'd even get hit a lot. But he never gave an inch."

The brush-back is to be expected, according to Winfield. "About 70 percent of the pitchers in the American League try to intimidate with the brush-back," he says.

How many really mean to hit a batter?

"One or two percent," Winfield estimates.

Most big leaguers subdue fear. They are able to conquer it. Tiger manager Sparky Anderson says the best he's seen at not being intimidated at the plate are Chet Lemon, Lee May, and Pete Rose.

"There are some players today," says Sparky, "who couldn't stand up to the rough, tough knock-'em-down pitching of 30 years ago. But Lemon, May, and Rose could handle the situation in any baseball era. All three of them had absolutely no fear up there at the plate."

★ ★ ★

Everybody in baseball knows you have to expect the unexpected at all times. You never know what might happen. For example, there was a play in a Cub-Dodger game during the 1916 season. Then-Dodger Casey Stengel is the authority for this one, and as Casey always said, "You can look it up."

It happened on a strikeout.

The Cubs were at Ebbets Field in Brooklyn. Their batter, Rollie Zeider, struck out. The pitch got by the Brooklyn catcher and hit the umpire, Mal Eason, in the chest. The ball rebounded toward third base. There Mike Mowrey, the Brooklyn third baseman, picked up the ball off the grass and fired it to first in time to retire the batter Zeider, running to first after he had fanned. A crazy, unexpected way to get a man out. And the Brooklyn third baseman, Mowrey, was credited with an assist on the strikeout.

★ ★ ★

Talk about a bad day—the old Brooklyn club had one on June 17, 1885. On that day, the Brooklyn American Association team—then considered a big league team—made 20 errors in one game. That's right, *20*. The team kicked a few out of pure ineptness, but most of the errors by Brooklyn in that game were made on purpose. The players didn't like the man they had pitching for them that afternoon, John Francis "Phenomenal" Smith.

After such a sorry exhibition, the club owner, Charley Byrne, called a meeting. He threatened to fine and suspend every Brooklyn player if things didn't improve. Next day they played errorless ball.

Phenomenal Smith also pitched in the majors for the Athletics, Pittsburgh, Detroit, Baltimore, and the Phillies. It was at Baltimore that he had his craziest seasonal record. In the 1887 season he won 25 games, but he also lost 30.

And Mr. Smith goes down in history as the player his teammates hated so much that they made 20 errors in one game behind his pitching.

Speaking My Piece

14

Times, They Are a Changin'

"The great trouble with baseball today is that most of the players are in the game for the money that's in it—not for the love of it, the excitement of it and the thrill of it. Times seem to have changed since I broke in more than a generation ago. I really believe that in those days, if a player had been forced to choose between a 50-percent cut in pay or complete retirement from the game, he would have taken the cut—and gladly."—Ty Cobb

As a statistic, the complete game is now about as useful as a cut-glass flyswatter or a fur-lined syrup pitcher.

There was a time when complete games were the norm. Jack Chesbro set the modern record with 48 for the New York Highlanders in 1904. Two years earlier, Vic Willis of Boston had set the National League record when he went the route in 45 starts.

Now, it's different. The top pitchers in complete games in 1993, for instance, were Chuck Finley of California (13) and Greg Maddux of the Braves (8). The only other pitcher with more than 10 was Kevin Brown of Texas with 12. Maddux's eight is the all-time record low for a leader in complete games for a full season.

You can blame the demise of the complete game on the modern-day managers. "Go out there and give me five or six good innings," the manager tells his starter. After that, it's the bullpen by committee. The manager removes his starter, brings in a setup man, makes another change or two, and then gets to his closer in the ninth.

All of this underscores the importance of the bullpen. Twenty years ago, most pitchers went to the bullpen as a punishment, or perhaps because they had a sore arm. The bullpen was the Siberia of the pitching world. Not anymore. Now, a reliever can be the star of the team and make more money than any of his teammates.

Still, I believe that as a matter of pride most pitchers would still rather start than relieve. The starter has more room for mistakes. A home run in the first or second inning might not harm him the way a home run would in the eighth or ninth.

"You come in to relieve in the ninth with a couple of guys on," Tigers reliever Mike Henneman said. "If the batter hits a line drive to the third baseman for a double play, you're a hero. But if that line drive goes a foot past the third baseman for a double, two runs score and you're a bum. That's the life of the reliever."

The main thrust is still to win. That's all that matters.

★ ★ ★

Several fans have asked me why relief pitchers (especially closers) can pitch only one or two innings per game without wearing out their arms and jeopardizing their careers.

I once put that question to two experts who were managing against each other, Roger Craig of the San Francisco Giants and Jeff Torborg of the New York Mets.

Craig was an outstanding major league pitcher and pitching coach before he became a manager. Many look on him as the top guru of modern-day pitching. Torborg, an ex-catcher, worked some of the game's top pitchers and is a student of bullpen handling.

Each of these experts told me that the modern big league reliever should never pitch more than two innings a game, if he is to be used on a regular basis.

"You can't allow your closer to over-extend himself," Craig said. "I know it sounds like babying, but throwing a baseball in a tight-game situation puts tremendous strain on a pitcher's arm."

"But," I asked him, "aren't these pitchers well-trained and well-conditioned athletes? Shouldn't they be able to pitch more than an inning or two at a time?"

"No," he answered. "A manager can't take the chance of ruining his pitcher's career."

Then Craig recalled an incident when he was pitching for the Dodgers.

"I went in to relieve and worked for two or three innings. After the game, an internationally known doctor from England came into our clubhouse. He had never before seen a baseball game.

"'I am amazed,' he told me, 'that you can put so much pressure on your arm. That motion is very unnatural and pulls your muscles and tendons out of kilter with every pitch.'

"The doctor told me that the only natural motion which wouldn't strain my arm was underhanded. I guess that's why softball pitchers last so long."

Torborg agrees with Craig.

"I'll never let my reliever go more than two or three innings. If he's my closer, I am going to restrict him to one or two at the most. I relented last week and let John Franco work three innings. Now, he's on the disabled list."

Torborg feels strongly that he must establish roles for his pitchers. "I like to let my man know that he is either going to work middle relief or be a closer. Once he knows, he can settle down and relax."

While coaching in New York, Torborg was instrumental in moving Dave Righetti from starting to the bullpen. "Fans don't understand," Torborg says. "They think we baby our closers. We are simply trying not to ruin their careers."

★ ★ ★

Baseball has not had a Triple Crown winner since Boston's Carl Yastrzemski in 1967. While checking on that, I discovered something that had escaped me. In 1933, there were two Triple Crown winners, and both came from the same city—Philadelphia. In the American League, Jimmie Foxx won the honor when he batted .356, hit 48 home runs, and knocked in 163 runs. Chuck Klein took the Triple Crown in the National League; he hit .368 with 28 home runs, and 120 RBIs.

If that double feat had happened in one city in our modern baseball era, there would be all kinds of excitement. The TV networks would break into their programming; ESPN would be churning out documentaries; and the headlines all over the nation would be screaming about Foxx and Klein.

To find out the impact of the double feat at the time, I checked the 1934 *Reach Baseball Guide*. In the first eight pages of articles, the editor didn't mention Foxx or Klein. In the American League review of the 1933 season, Foxx' accomplishment was ignored. The National League review noted that Klein "led the league in batting and also took hitting honors."

When the averages were analyzed, there were mentions of the two sluggers. One article pointed out that Foxx hit three home runs in one game and twice had five hits in a game. However, there was never any use of the term Triple Crown. In review, I'd have to say that Klein and Foxx winning the Triple Crown in the same city was no big deal for their contemporaries.

For Foxx, winning the Triple Crown also led to his selection as the American League's Most Valuable Player for the second straight season. Klein didn't fare as well; in the National League, the MVP went to New York Giants pitching great Carl Hubbell, who led the league with 23 wins, 10 shutouts, and a 1.66 ERA in $308\frac{2}{3}$ innings.

Klein was traded to the Cubs before the 1934 season and never again matched his exploits with the Phils. Foxx was unloaded to the Red Sox in 1936, continued his slugging there, and finished with the Cubs and Phillies.

Jimmie's Triple Crown season of 1933 was no help to him financially. Connie Mack asked him that winter to take a pay cut from $16,333 to $12,000. Only after long and tough negotiations was Foxx finally able to maintain his salary. Like the *Reach Baseball Guide*, Connie Mack felt that the Triple Crown—at least in the pocketbook—was no big deal.

If two sluggers from the same city won the Triple Crown in our times, it would be more than a big deal. It would be a sensation.

★ ★ ★

Dave Winfield, Robin Yount, and George Brett are the most recent superstars to pass the 3,000-hit mark.

There wasn't a whole lot of hoopla about these stars hitting that magic number. I had the thought that Brett attracted a lot more media attention in 1980 when he was flirting with a .400 batting average (he finished at .390). I asked him about that.

"Yes," he told me. "When I was hitting .400, I had a lot more attention. I think it was because nobody had hit .400 in a long time (Ted Williams with his .406 in 1941), and the 3,000-hit mark had been reached by several players in recent years."

Next I checked with another superstar, one who had also banged out 3,000 hits, almost hit .400, and made the

Hall of Fame: Rod Carew, batting coach of the California Angels. I asked him to compare the attention he received when almost hitting .400 (he finished the '77 season at .388) and when he got his 3,000th.

"There was much more pressure to hit .400." he said. "The goal of 3,000 hits was a definite one and we all knew, barring injury, I would reach it. The .400 average was more touch-and-go."

Carew said that when he neared the .400 mark, he ceased to have fun playing the game. "It really got bad," he said. "The media crush was too much. I told my manager, Gene Mauch, that I would come to the park early and try to meet the press, but after 3:30 I wouldn't see anyone because I had to concentrate on the game."

In the early baseball days, records didn't attract the attention they do now. Sam Rice, the talented Washington outfielder, was only 13 hits short of 3,000 when he quit the game. In his final year at Cleveland, he played in 97 games and batted .293. Certainly he could have played a few more years.

Even stranger is the case of Sam Crawford, the long-time Tigers' outfielder. Sam had 2,964 hits when he left the major league scene. However, at the age of 38, he went to the minors. He played four years for Los Angeles in the Pacific Coast League, collecting 781 hits over that period.

Can you imagine such a thing happening in modern baseball?

★ ★ ★

One winter in Rome, I became friendly with a gentleman from the CIA. He told me a story about the tribal feuds in Yemen. It seems that the tribes there engaged in deadly sport. Each tribe selected one of its warriors. The men were put on a starting line and their heads were severed with a hot sword. The warrior who fell forward the greater distance won the game for his tribe.

My comment: "Some sport. And probably the only one where the ex-athlete doesn't retire and become a TV or radio announcer."

All of which brings up one of the questions asked of me most frequently: "How do you feel about former players entering the announcing profession?" I welcomed anybody into the announcing profession. I didn't and don't think there should be restrictions. The only criterion should be: Can he get the job done? Let's judge it on that basis and on that basis alone. The ex-athlete has a decided advantage over the so-called professional announcer trying to break in. His reputation as a player is a guarantee that the listening public will accept him as an authority. He has been in the limelight for several years and already is a hero, so the public will accept him more readily than a professional announcer. Also, he is allowed the luxury of learning on the job, a luxury the other type cannot enjoy.

Many of the ex-athletes have done great jobs as announcers. They have worked hard, studied their new profession, and become successful. Some have slipped by with little homework and little application to the job. But isn't this also true among the professional announcers?

The invasion of the booth by ballplayers is nothing new. Jack Graney, the Cleveland outfielder, was broadcasting long before most of the current announcers were born. Some of the other early ex-player broadcasters were Walter Johnson, Lew Fonseca, Charlie Grimm, Rogers Hornsby, Frankie Frisch, and the Tigers' great Harry Heilmann. And don't forget that umpire Dolly Stark used to be a baseball broadcaster—the only one I remember from the umpiring ranks.

When I came into the major leagues in 1948 there were only a few ex-player broadcasters. On the other hand, there were only 16 major league clubs. And each club had only two announcers.

Now, with league expansion, many more jobs are available. Also, there is TV now. So each team's announcing crew numbers at least three and sometimes four or five.

Thus, despite the increased influx of players, the number of broadcasting jobs for the professionals is still about the same. But competition is still fierce and it is very difficult to land a job.

I sympathize with the announcer who has worked several years or even many years in the minors only to find he is shut out of a major league job because the team, the sponsor, or the station wants an ex-player. Yet many such announcers make it. I feel there is room for both types—as long as they can get the job done.

★ ★ ★

If you're going to be part of the baseball media you had better get used to The Gulf.

There always has been and always will be a gulf between the uniformed personnel and the media. It is a gulf created by suspicion on the part of the players and enhanced more recently by their tremendous salaries.

I suppose this gulf persists in other sports. But I know that it is very evident in baseball.

In my broadcasting career I have been with the players in all sorts of situations. I have shagged flies with them; played golf; eaten meals; sat in bars; ridden buses, trains, and planes; entertained them in my home; been a guest in their homes; written articles and songs with them; entered into business transactions; and gotten to know their families. Yes, I've done just about everything with the players. Still, because I have not been a member of the team, I cannot crack that barrier. The Gulf is always there.

The players have trusted me. I've often been taken into their confidence, but my persona remains different from that of a teammate.

I am not alone in that regard. I find it true with all

members of the media. I'm older now and at 76 don't pal around with 22-year-old players. Yet, I see young reporters who do, and it is no different for them.

One particular writer always used to come to the park very early, sit in the dugout, chew his tobacco like a player. He would joke around with the guys, socialize with them, and try to be part of the crowd. But even he had to face The Gulf.

The problem pertains even to ex-players. A certain broadcaster might have once played for the team he is now covering. Many of the players were his close teammates. He lived with them six months each year. Still, once he becomes a member of the media, he too must contend with The Gulf. He is no longer a member of the fraternity. He is now an announcer and, regardless of his past association, is now not completely trusted by anyone who wears the uniform.

The Gulf has always been with us. However, it is wider now. When I came to the major leagues in 1948 there was more of a closeness between the players and the media. Reporters covered only the games. They didn't visit the clubhouses, looking for quotes. They rode the trains with the players, drank with them, and did not write a lot of things they saw the players do. Investigative reporting by sportswriters very seldom took place in those days.

Today, the reporters are forced by television and radio to go beyond the game in their reportage. Most fans know the score and the details of a game as soon as it is over. These fans want more information than some straight report. So, we see the reporters coming very early to the ballpark, staying late, hounding the players and managers for inside stories. They are not satisfied to write what happened; they also want to know, and almost need to know, why it happened. That approach, that desire for more information, is certainly part of the game—but it just makes The Gulf wider than ever.

★ ★ ★

People ask me if I have a special philosophy about broadcasting ballgames. My basic concept is that fans tune in for the game. The game is paramount. The announcer is secondary.

The game should be announced in simple English. Call it as simply as you can. Any additions—any embroidery you put on it—are extra. But first of all, call the game and do the additional things afterward.

I tried to stay away from statistics. I had to say such things as batting averages, home runs, and his runs-batted-in the first time a guy came up. I didn't even like to use those, but I knew people demanded them.

As I got older and more experienced, I used fewer and fewer statistics. I think they're a crutch for a lot of announcers. On the radio, for instance, I don't think most listeners can follow all those numbers. I've heard guys say when somebody comes in that he's making his 22nd appearance and that he has pitched 22 innings, given up 16 runs, 28 hits, 18 walks, and has 19 strikeouts...and by the time you've given two figures, you've lost your listeners.

So my concept was that I was talking to a person—a composite person—somebody who was interested in baseball or maybe somebody who wasn't. You've got a college professor, a six-year-old who is just starting to learn about the game, a fellow who might have played professional baseball, and a lady who is 96. You've got somebody who doesn't know much about the Tigers and somebody who is steeped in Tiger tradition. You've got all kinds listening in, and you have to hit somewhere in the middle of all these people.

There were some nights when everything came easy. The next night, for no apparent reason, you'd have all kinds of trouble. You could make the same amount of preparation and have the same amount of rest, but the game was a struggle for you.

I've talked to other announcers about this, and it's hard to explain why some nights are easy and some nights are difficult. There is no pattern to it. It doesn't depend on how the game is going or even how you feel. It just happens, and I guess the best way to put it is that this is just a human reaction. Some days are just better than others, though I don't think the public can discern this the way you can yourself.

I was able to keep my enthusiasm because each game was different. It was fun for me to go to the ballpark. I've always enjoyed baseball. Each game presented a different challenge because I had to sit down and react to what was happening on the field. As soon as a ball was pitched, I had to have words come out of my mouth—via my brain, I hope—on what was going on. It was a challenge to react to everything, no matter what the score was.

My job required immediate responses, so I would sort of play the game as it went along. I tried to respond in an artistic sense to what I was seeing.

I believed in giving the score a lot. I liked to give the other scores as much as possible, too. I figured somebody from Ohio might be driving through Michigan, and he'd like to know how the Reds were doing. Yet, some people would write in and say, "Hey, why do you give all those scores and interrupt the game?"

I liked broadcasting home games the best. That's because I worked in a great booth in Tiger Stadium and also because the fans were cheering at the right time. I loved it when I could let the crowd do the talking for me. When we were on the road and Lou Whitaker hit a three-run homer, I was the only one who got excited. The ballpark was silent. At home, the fans gave us a lift.

Sometimes I think there are too many distractions in the ballpark.

I think people are there for the games, and the beauty of baseball is that they can sit down and relax and talk to each other between the pitches. Silence is golden. I even tried to give them some silence on the air.

As much as I like music, I don't think the ballpark is a place to have music going on all the time. It's like going into a restaurant to have an nice meal and visit with a friend, and the music is so loud you can't even hear yourself think.

I guess after 50 years in the booth I have a few opinions on how baseball should be announced. But, however you call it, it's still a great game.

★ ★ ★

You read and hear a lot about rude players refusing to sign their names for begging kids. Critics usually blast the player or celebrity for high-handed treatment of the fans. But the players and other autographers have rights, too.

Often the autograph seeker is rude and pushy. Sometimes he won't even have a pen. I've seen players' sports coats ruined with squirts of ink and torn by crowds trying to close in for autographs.

I understand the difficulties of the situation. Players make enemies by turning down autograph requests. On the other hand, the autograph seekers are sometimes overdemanding and unfair to the players.

Collectors who market autographs have soured the players.

"I don't mind signing," Tiger Dave Bergman told me. "But often I know a dealer has sent kids to me for an autograph he will sell."

Another problem develops when a large crowd gathers. If a player signs one autograph, he'll have to stay and sign 200. He may have someone waiting for him or he may be in a hurry to get somewhere. It's not always possible to stop and accommodate everybody.

Here's a familiar scene. At 2 A.M., the Tigers' bus pulls

up in front of a New York hotel. Waiting at the entrance is
a group of eight or 10 people of all ages with photographs
and autograph books.

A sequel: The team bus is leaving for Yankee Stadium.
The same group has surrounded the bus. Fifty minutes
later the bus arrives at Yankee Stadium. Yes, the same collectors have made the 20-mile trip and beaten the bus to the
ballpark. They are waiting again with pens in hand. Are
they loyal fans or sharp hustlers out for the buck? You can
understand how the players can become hardened to the
situation.

All major leaguers receive autograph requests in the
mail. Most of them sign, if the sender includes a stamped,
self-addressed envelope. It's a real burden for the stars because they are inundated with cards, photos, and other
items.

Some of the Hall-of-Famers refuse to sign cards, but
most of them are accommodating. Al Kaline estimates that
he receives about 40 requests each day.

Some of the stars ask that the sender donate $3 to $5 to
charity.

What we all need is some politeness, decency, and common sense. Most players will cooperate if they are approached in the correct way. Most fans are understanding.
Let's try to get both sides together over this thorny and
complicated problem of autographs.

★ ★ ★

Major league playoffs are a hot topic these days. But
baseball playoffs are nothing new. They started in the minors in 1933 and were the brainchild of Frank Shaughnessy,
business manager of the Montreal Royals.

Frank derived the idea from hockey and convinced the
International League to use his plan. It was a success, pro-
viding interest in the final weeks of the season and a boost

in attendance. Other leagues followed the Shaughnessy plan, and it is now a part of baseball history.

However, the lower minors had used various gimmicks to save a runaway season even before that. One of those ideas, contrived by the Southern League, ruined my boyhood summer of 1928.

I was 10 and had been following my hometown heroes, the Atlanta Crackers, for two seasons. The Crackers didn't play well in the first few months of 1928. The Birmingham Barons, their hated rivals, had raced to a large lead by midseason.

In their combined wisdom, the league owners voted to split the season. They sensed a runaway for the Barons and a large drop in attendance. Now it was established that the teams would begin a new season in July, and the second-half winner would battle the Barons for the pennant in a playoff.

My team, the Crackers, began to roll. They took the league lead, and it seemed certain that they would win the second half and meet Birmingham for the championship. One Saturday night, I went to bed happy because my Crackers were on top.

The next morning, I was shocked by headlines telling me that the Crackers dropped into last place. It seems that the hated Barons blew the whistle on the Crackers. The Southern League rules stated that each team could have only so many "A" players (players with certain experience) on their rosters. The Atlanta club had been using too many "A" players in its drive to first place.

So the league ruled that 14 Cracker victories be turned into losses. That dropped the Crackers all the way to eighth place.

My most vivid memory of that summer of 1928 is opening the sports section on that certain Sunday morning to find that my heroes were no longer leading the league. It was the greatest shock I've ever experienced as a baseball fan.

15

Will Baseball
Survive?

"Baseball and malaria keep coming back." —Gene Mauch

The 1993 World Series put a glaring spotlight on two of baseball's most harmful developments—the designated hitter rule and the inordinate length of games.

I've seen many changes in baseball since I came to the major leagues in 1948. Most of them have been improvements; but these two have been detrimental. The DH rule might be all right if it were used in both leagues. It does add an offensive thrust and it keeps around some of the good hitters who can't handle their fielding responsibilities anymore. However, it makes a joke of World Series play and certainly has penalized the American League team, which must depend on its pitchers to bat when many of them have not swung at a pitch since their high school days.

The DH takes away strategy from the managers in the American League during the season. When October rolls around, the league is also penalized by not being allowed to use a hitter around whom an entire attack has been built.

The Toronto Blue Jays' Paul Molitor could not DH in

199

last year's Series after he had done it for 170 games during the season and the playoffs.

"It's a distraction," Molitor said. "We go all year without having to worry about it and now that we're playing for the world championship, it becomes a problem we have to address."

The Series saw Toronto manager Cito Gaston bench John Olerud, the league batting champion, in one game and later play his ex-DH Molitor at third base, a position Paul had not played in three years.

"It's a bad situation," Gaston said. "You should not have to switch back and forth like that, depending on which park you're playing in. Also, it's an advantage for the National League team. They don't have to make an adjustment. We do. It's not fair. It's not right."

Baseball should abandon the DH, or at least insist that both the National League and the American League use it. The current situation where the National League refuses to go along with the rule is ridiculous. High schools, colleges, the minors—all of baseball—uses the DH, but not the National League.

One of the ironies of the DH is that it was first proposed by National League president John Heydler in the early 1930s. Fans all over the country reacted strongly against the plan. National League club executives were either cool or indifferent. The DH met its stiffest opposition in the American League. The league called it "damnfoolery."

For many years, nobody thought about the DH. Then in 1973, it was adopted. Its champion this time, again, had been a league president—the American League's Joe Cronin.

Criticism for the DH has been mixed since the rule was introduced in 1973. But criticisms of the extended time of games has grown over the last two or three seasons into a groundswell that now includes even baseball's staunchest defenders.

The length of games has gotten out of hand. Once

again, we saw the World Series make that point so vividly. The fourth game of the Series, in Philadelphia, lasted four hours and 14 minutes—a Series record. Yes, it was an exciting game, but few were around to watch it end, either in person or on TV.

The marathon showed all of us that some remedy is needed for the problem of the overlong game. Like everyone else, I have my list. First of all, the strike zone should be larger. I have often talked to the umpires about this.

"Why don't you call strikes by the book?" I ask. "Then you'd see hitters hitting more pitches and the game would move along faster."

Their answer: "If we did that, the batters would be squawking at us all the time."

"So what?" is my reply. "They're going to gripe about something anyway. And if you establish a correct strike zone and use it consistently, sooner or later the bitching will stop."

Another remedy is to make the batter stay in the batter's box. Now they move away from the plate, take practice swings, and make the pitcher wait on them. Then, the pitcher is not ready. He steps off the mound, and a contest begins as to who will be ready for the other.

Mention this to the umpires and they protest.

"We can't take a chance that a batter might get hurt. We have to call time and let him step away," they say.

I disagree. I don't think the hitter is that much endangered. Keep him at the plate and move the game along.

Another way to speed up the game is to eliminate conferences. I mean those inane moments when as early as the first inning the pitching coach, or the catcher, will amble out toward the mound and engage the pitcher in conversation. Can't these pearls of wisdom be dropped between innings? Or, if it's so urgent, let the coach, catcher, or manager yell or give a signal to the pitcher.

I suggested elimination of conferences in *The Sporting*

News many years ago. After the idea was printed, the Washington Senators' general manager George Selkirk wrote a scathing letter to the editor of *The Sporting News*.

"If Ernie Harwell had ever played in the major leagues, he would know that conferences have to be a part of the game," he wrote. But he did not tell us why they have to be a part of the game. I still maintain we can do without them.

There are other remedies to the lengthy game; but most of them have been bandied about in print for years. I used to think that only the media was concerned with the length of games. Now, I've come around to realizing that the fans object also.

Baseball has to address the problem of the long game. And it has to do something about the DH rule.

★ ★ ★

Baseball is a survivor.

In a jungle of media carping, inadequate ownership, exorbitant player salaries, and competition from other sports, the grand old game just keeps on keeping on. It seems that no matter how often baseball shoots itself in the foot, the true fan still appreciates its beauty and endurance. Its intrinsic qualities are so strong that nothing seems to truly bother baseball.

I compare it in a way to the church. The church has survived for centuries despite all the sins and crimes which have been committed in its name. It survives because of great inner strength and a firm foundation.

Baseball is like that—albeit in a lesser sense.

I know. I'm prejudiced. Baseball has been a large part of my life—and will continue to be. I've loved it since I saw my first game at old Ponce de Leon Park in Atlanta at the age of eight. I've defended it throughout my life.

When I was in grammar school, I read in the annual baseball guides that baseball was losing its grip on the national psyche. One year tennis was the game that would replace baseball. Next season it might be softball, or then golf. Later—in the 1950s and '60s—pro football became the sport in fashion. And more lately, it's been basketball. But baseball survives.

Baseball's strength is the game itself, the game on the playing field. Its major weakness lies in the fact that it has become too big a business. Its greed stands in the way of progress. Yet baseball has been a business since it became a professional sport more than 120 years ago. Part of its problem is that the partners in this business, i.e., the owners, are in the awkward position of being not only partners, but also rivals.

Baseball on the field today remains strong. I don't think I've seen so many fine young players in one season as I saw in my last year broadcasting in the American League. Young men of great talent like Ken Griffey, Jr., Frank Thomas, John Olerud, Juan Gonzalez, Carlos Baerga, Kenny Lofton, Travis Fryman, and Roberto Alomar have shown critics that baseball can still attract great young athletes.

In the National League, look at youngsters like Barry Bonds, Larry Walker, Moises Alou, Marquis Grissom, Jose Rijo, Darryl Kile, Steve Avery, John Smoltz, Mike Piazza, and Carlos Garcia. These young men point up the fact that the player of today is bigger, stronger, and faster than the average player of earlier eras.

Many old-timers say that the players of today don't hustle because they make too much money and have long-time contracts. A common observation is that many don't put out unless they are into the final year of a contract. I heard the same criticism in another form many years ago. In those days it was couched in the term "salary drive," a phrase hung on a player's extra effort in September.

A few years ago G.H. Fleming wrote a book, *The Dizziest Season*. His concept was to quote contemporary baseball reporters for each day of 1934, from January 1 through December 31. In one of his excerpts he quoted a sportswriter this way: "No wonder the players don't hustle these days. They have three-year contracts and they're making $3,000 a year."

Almost any other denigration of baseball today finds its antecedents in years past. Take a long look at a few of these examples:

"The players of today are not a bit like those of my day. In my day, such a little thing as a charley horse, a sprain... or a bad hand would not keep a man out of the game. Now, they get out for the least thing and stay out when to all appearances, they are able to play ball." (Jimmy Manning, 1901)

"Baseball has been degenerating for the past 10 years. If a game such as used to be played in the time of Kelly, Clarkson, Welch, Foutz and Caruthers were played now, the people who saw it would go wild." (Charles Comiskey, 1902)

"No clan of men on the face of the globe earn their money easier than the professional baseball players, as they work two hours a day when they work at all...Still, they are constantly complaining of being overworked and they have to be coaxed and humored like a lot of spoiled children..." (*The National Police Gazette*, 1886)

Some of baseball critics want it both ways. They attack the game when it resists change; and they also attack it when it tries to progress through change.

This two-way attack is exemplified in the reaction to baseball's effort to come up with a three-divisional playoff. Those who objected to the idea felt that the game was losing its "purity" with such a playoff plan. Yet, when the game makes no move, it is called "stodgy" and "old-fashioned."

I like the new plan. It will perk up the month of September. There is no excitement in any city or state like that generated by having a team in a pennant race—whether for the top spot in a division or for second place. Football, basketball, and hockey have proved that.

If people want "purity," they have to take us back to baseball with two major leagues of eight teams each, no major league cities west of St. Louis, and no great black stars. I don't want to retreat that far.

Another criticism of modern baseball is that it doesn't have the kinds of characters that made the game so colorful. That criticism took a beating last season when the Philadelphia Phils became the National League champions. The Broad Street Bellies, with their shaggy hair, torn uniforms, lusty appetites, and down-and-dirty demeanor became the darlings of the media. The experts went all the way back to the Depression-era '30s to compare them to the St. Louis Gashouse Gang.

In many directions baseball is prospering. Attendance is soaring. Minor league franchises, which several years ago were almost free for the asking, are now bringing million-dollar price tags. Collectors have bid prices of mementoes and autographs to record highs. Fantasy camps flourish and Fantasy Baseball is a whole new area of fan interest.

Critics say that youngsters have no interest in the game. Yet, much of my mail is from those under 15, and when I go to the various ballparks I see hordes of young people enjoying the games.

Yes, baseball is still great. Right now the game's foremost task is to achieve a feeling of unity between the owners and the players. These two groups should realize that each has something fantastic. There is prosperity for both. The two groups should sit down and tell each other that they both want to help the game go forward—even if that requires some sort of compromise.

★ ★ ★

It was the final Baltimore Orioles series of the 1959 season. I had broadcast the Orioles-Yankees game at Yankee Stadium that Friday night and had returned to my room in the Roosevelt Hotel. The phone rang.

"Hi, Ernie," said the voice. "It's George Kell in Detroit. The Tigers want you for their new announcer."

That was the start of my Tigers career. I ended that career last October, when I broadcast the Tiger-Yankee game
from Yankee Stadium.

Between that phone call and that final broadcast, it has
been more than just fun and games. It has been a great life
with many thrills and only a few regrets.

As the man on TV says, "We've got highlights." So, at
random I'm listing some observations, thoughts and
memories that have touched me over those 34 seasons. Not
in any necessary order, I'll remember:

My first Tigers spring training in Lakeland, 1960. We
had rented a house on Comanche Trail, but the boys were
ashamed of our eight-year-old Rambler and got out of the
car a block before we reached the house…

Old-fashioned Henley Field. Trainer Jack Homel and
his mongoose, a crudely stuffed animal that snapped out of
a box and scared the unsuspecting…The Kuenn-Colavito
trade. Rick Ferrell announced it the final day of spring
training, and we all thought it was a practical joke…The
bubble eyes of Bill DeWitt, whose one-year Tigers' reforma-
tion ended in his abrupt firing…The cool dignity of owner
John Fetzer…

The night in 1973 when I inadvertently postponed the
California game. Driving away from the stadium, I heard
Ray Lane say, "Ernie, come back wherever you are." The
game was resumed and the Tigers won…

The 1971 All-Star Game at Tiger Stadium. I announced
the pregame ceremonies and then watched from the third
deck in right field. What a thrill to see Reggie Jackson's tremendous home run head for that transformer on the right
center-field roof!

Golf on the road with George Kell, my first Tigers'
partner…The shyness and innate goodness of Al Kaline…
The pleasant personality of Bob Scheffing, a personality
that belied his nickname of Grumpy…Doing the on-the-
field eulogy of Charlie Dressen after he had died in mid-
season 1966.…

The riot in '67 and the bitter end to the Tigers' pennant chase. They split doubleheaders the final two days, and Boston slipped in to win the pennant... Jose Feliciano's national anthem before the fifth game of the 1968 World Series, and all the furor that followed...

Denny McLain, playing the organ and kidding around the night before the '68 World Series opener in St. Louis... The intimidation of Cards pitcher Bob Gibson in that Series...And how Mickey Lolich beat the unbeatable Gibson in the seventh game...

The time I rode that tiny plane with Sonny Eliot and John Butsacaris to Boston. They took me there to broadcast Bucky Dent's home run that beat the Red Sox in the '78 playoff...Broadcasting the '63 World Series with Joe Garagiola. We got paid per game, and the Dodgers swept the Yankees in four...Another broadcast thrill, working the '61 All-Star Game, the only one that ended in a tie...

Jim Campbell calling me in Florida to tell me I'd been named to the Baseball Hall of Fame at Cooperstown... Paul Carey's courage during the 1984 Series when he found out his wife, Patty, had an inoperable brain tumor... Writing the song "Move Over Babe" with Tigers pitcher Bill Slayback...His wife, Robin, played rhythm on the demo record by shaking 15 pennies in a jar...

My father figure, Charles Kuralt of CBS-TV, telling me he used to listen to me broadcast the Atlanta Crackers games when he was a youngster...The loyalty of engineer Howard Stitzel...Emceeing Al Kaline Day and being there when the numbers of Charlie Gehringer and Hank Greenberg were retired...

Frank Tanana's shutout pitching in the '87 clincher against Toronto...Three great Tigers home run hitters: Colavito, Gibson, and Fielder...The overpowering noise at the Metrodome when the Twins beat the Tigers...Good times in the American League pressrooms...Popcorn in the middle three innings...

That 22-inning game, won by the Yankees on Jackie Reed's only major league home run...Guesting on the "Larry King Show" and "Good Morning America"...The joy of seeing a rookie's success, and the sadness of watching a veteran cut...

Dave Bergman's quiet dedication...Alan Trammell's class...Driving off the Lodge Freeway and seeing Tiger Stadium loom like a big, gray battleship...Dinner in New York at D'Angelos with Alex Grammas, and almost going to sleep during the Broadway performance of *Cats*...The infectious spirit of Tony Taylor...Umpire Rocky Roe's friendly grin...The deep Texas laugh of Durwood Merrill... Jeff Torborg's thoughtfulness and his help when I was one of the writers of the book, *Scouting Report*...

Herbie Redmond, the dancing groundskeeper...The enthusiasm of Joe "The Brow" Diroff...Max Raimi, the Chicago Symphony viola player, who would not buy a house in Chicago until he found out that he could pick up the Tigers' radio broadcast at that location...

Our family's winter in Spain. When we landed at Metro Airport the customs officer told me I was no longer on TV and had a new radio partner, Gene Osborn...The feet-on-the-ground outlook of Walt Terrell...John McNamara, the Angels' manager, crying at my Baseball Chapel presentation...Speeches at small-town churches and civic clubs...Cruising on the Q.E.II with Brooks Robinson, Stan Musial, Roger Craig, and Monte Irvin... Eulogizing three great friends at their funerals—Hal Middlesworth, Elsie Nemeth, and Ollie McLaughlin... Frank Tanana's Christian concern for his friends and teammates...The valued counsel of lawyer Gary Spicer...

Proposing, during my broadcast, for two bashful suitors... Meeting their wives and babies years later at Tiger Stadium...Ernie's Breakfast Club...Those ladies who took trips to Tigers out-of-town games and treated me to breakfast...Visiting the umpires and being invited to rub up baseballs for a game...Norm Cash's funeral. I flew in from the playoffs in Boston and almost missed the graveside service...The joy of having the family at Cooperstown, New York, for my Hall-of-Fame speech—my most nervous moment...Testifying at a Billy Graham crusade in Tampa... Homer and Jethro, the RCA song-comedy team, visiting the booth and telling me they would record my song, "Upside Down."

Bert Campaneris throwing his bat at Lerrin LaGrow in the '72 playoffs....Charlie Finley's mule...Billy Martin's temper and his drive to self-destruction...M.C. Hammer, then a 13-year-old clubhouse worker, bringing us the lineups in Oakland...Visits to the White House. President Ronald Reagan, telling me how he broadcast baseball and football. Vice President George Bush using my photo in his presidential campaign literature...Salutes in 1991 around the league...Pitching to Lance Parrish in Anaheim, California...Tossing another first ball in Seattle...My video tribute at County Stadium, Milwaukee, and all the other lunches and speeches around the league...

Those are great memories. But most of all I cherish the remembrance I have of Tigers fans everywhere, especially here in Michigan. I remember:

Tony Hawley, a 13-year old in Belding, wrote me a three-page letter in December of 1990 after I had been fired. He said: "Ernie, if you ever need a place to stay, a job, or some money, or even an organ (you know, like a kidney), I'm here to help"...

And Sarah Simpson, that wonderful lady who runs the press elevator at Tiger Stadium, told me during the 1991 season: "No wonder you're happy. Most people have to die to have good things said or written about them. But now before you die, you've already found how much all of us love you"...

Yes, it's been fun. And I thank all of you for the memories.

Afterword

16

Moments in Time

*"The rhythms of the game are so similar to the patterns
of American Life. Periods of leisure, interrupted
by bursts of frantic activity."*—Roger Kahn

*Author's Note: I leave you with some of the most memorable and
dramatic moments of my broadcasting career, as I called them over
the air.*

July 8, 1958
All-Star Game at Baltimore

So we go down to that full count, now three-and-two
with two out and nobody on…4-3, the American League in
the lead in the ninth inning and Crandall up there against
Billy O'Dell…Now the windup by O'Dell. The pitch is
swung on and popped up over near second base—Fox
backs up on the grass in right—he's under it—he's got it
and the game is over. The American Leaguers win it.

October 6, 1963
Game 4, World Series
New York at Los Angeles

Now it's all between Koufax and Hector Lopez—an error charged to Tracewski, the second baseman, for drop-
ping the throw from Maury Wills, the shortstop, on the

force play. It's a tap back past the mound to Maury Wills—he grabs it, throws to first—it's all over! The Dodgers win it!

September 14, 1968
Denny McLain's 30th Win
Oakland at Detroit

A man on first and a man on third, one man down, 2-2 the count on Willie Horton. Here's the set by Segui, here's the pitch. Swung on—a drive to left, that'll be the ballgame! It's over the head of Gosger! McLain wins his 30th! Here comes Stanley in to score. Willie Horton has singled and the ballgame is over. The Tigers win it, 5-4. Denny McLain is one of the first out of the dugout, racing out, and Horton is mobbed as the Tigers come from behind, and McLain has his 30th victory of the 1968 season.

September 17, 1968
Tigers Clinch Pennant
New York at Detroit

Well, this big crowd here ready to break loose. Three men on, two out, game tied, 1-1, in the ninth inning... McDaniel checking his sign with Jake Gibbs. The tall right-hander ready to go to work again. And the windup, and the pitch. He swings—a line shot, base hit, right field! The Tigers win it! Here comes Kaline to score! And it's all over! Don Wert singles! The Tigers mob Don. Kaline has scored, the fans are streaming on the field, and the Tigers have won their first pennant since nineteen-hundred-and-forty-five! Let's listen to the bedlam here at Tiger Stadium!

October 2, 1968
Game 1, World Series
Detroit at St. Louis

Gibson has tied the record of Sandy Koufax—15 strikeouts in a single World Series game. Trying for number 16 right now against Cash to break the record. He takes his set position, he delivers, here's the pitch. Swing and a miss! He did it!

October 10, 1968
Game 7, World Series
Detroit at St. Louis

Now the set by Gibson. We're ready. There's a swing and a flyball to center—here comes Flood digging hard. He almost fell down. It's over his head for a hit—Cash is rounding third—he scores. Willie Horton rounds third—he scores. Northrup goes on to third base, Detroit leads, 2-0.

July 15, 1973
Nolan Ryan's Second No-Hitter
Texas at Detroit

Now, Nolan Ryan is only one strike away from a no-hit performance…Only one strike away from tying the American League strikeout record by Bob Feller…Here's the windup—he pitches…Swing and a pop fly back into left field…going back is Meoli. He's there—makes the catch. Ryan has his no-hitter, but he does not tie the strikeout record. He is mobbed by his Angel teammates as he comes off the mound, and it is a no-hit victory by this young man from Texas.

October 2, 1978
One-Game Playoff for the American League East Pennant
New York at Boston

He's back in there choking the bat, waiting on the 1-1 pitch from Torrez.

Two men on. Two men out…2-0 Boston. And the pitch is on the way. He swings. There's a flyball to left field…Yastrzemski looking back, and that one is gone—a three-run homer for Bucky Dent and the Yankees have the lead. Just into the screen.

Bucky Dent hits a three-run homer for the Yankees, and

they go out in front of the Boston Red Sox here at Fenway Park. That one got in the screen by a couple of feet. Yastrzemski could do nothing but look up and watch it drift in there and the Yankees, after trailing, 2-0, take the lead, 3-2 ,in the seventh inning.

October 3, 1979
Game 1, American League Championship Series
California at Baltimore

Three runs, seven hits for California...Three runs, five hits for Baltimore...Base hit right here would win it—the right kind. Here's Montague—he pitches. There's a flyball to left—it's slicing—it may be—it's deep and it is a home run! A three-run homer for Lowenstein and the Orioles win the game in the 10th inning, 6-3. The Oriole team comes out to mob Lowenstein as he rounds third and heads home with the blow that wins the game and puts the Birds one up on their rivals from California.

April 15, 1983
Milt Wilcox' Near-Perfect Game
Detroit at Chicago

What a performance Wilcox has put on—two down in the ninth inning—the Tigers lead Chicago, 6-0. Twenty-six batters in a row have gone down before the slants of Wilcox. Hairston has zero hits in six trips on the season...looks for his first one...the crowd on its feet. The pitch—he swings—base hit! Center field! Hairston spoils the bid! A grimace by Wilcox on the mound and Hairston brings the ball through the middle for a single...taking the no-hit per-fect-game bid out of the grasp of Wilcox at the very last dra-matic moment.

April 7, 1984
Jack Morris' No-Hitter
Detroit at Chicago

One ball, two strikes, Morris ahead of the hitter.

Stegman back to first base. Bergman playing very wide of the bag on him. A tug of the cap by Morris. Working off the set position now. He goes to his set, Kittle waits. Here it comes—he struck him out and Morris has a no-hitter! Lance Parrish goes out and grabs him, and the Tigers get a no-hit performance for the first time since 1958 when Jim Bunning did it! Jack Morris, the no-hit hero, surrounded by his teammates. In the ninth for Chicago: no runs, no hits, no errors, one man left. And the final score, Detroit 4, Chicago 0!

October 14, 1984
Game 5, World Series
San Diego at Detroit
Ball one on Kirk. Here's the pitch. He swings, and there's a long drive to right! And it is a home run for Gibson! A three-run homer! The Tigers lead it, 8-4, in the eighth inning!

October 15, 1986
Game 7, American League Championship Series
California at Boston
Three-and-two with two down. Four-nothing, Boston, in the fourth…Now the set, Rice waits—the pitch. He swings—there's a flyball to left! It's deep! Going back is Downing—looking—it is long gone! A home run for Rice! A three-run homer, and a 7-0 lead for the Boston Red Sox in the fourth inning!

Index

A

Aaron, Henry, 115, 134
Aber, Al, 156
Abbott, Glen, 170
Ackerman, Carl, 95
Aguirre, Hank, 103
Albom, Mitch, 9
Allen, Mel, 14
Alexander, Grover, 5
Alomar, Roberto, 203
Alou, Moises, 203
Ames, Leon, 147
Amole, Doc, 148
Anderson, Sparky, 6, 69, 135, 182
Anson, Cap, 107
Aparicio, Luis, 154, 155
Appling, Luke, 67-68
Argyros, George, 23-24
Arlin, Harold, 5
Armour, William, 55
Averill, Earl, 104-106
Avery, Steve, 203

B

Baerga, Carlos, 203
Bahnsen, Stan, 136
Bailey, Ed, 139
Bair, Doug, 170
Baker, Del, 55
Baker, Frank, 160
Baldwin, Charles (Lady), 58
Bancroft, Francis Carter, 27-28
Banks, Ernie, 67

Barber, Steve, 154-155
Barrett, Jimmy, 65
Bauer, Hank, 154
Bavasi, Emil (Buzzie), 87
Baylor, Don, 39, 182
Belanger, Mark, 155
Belinsky, Bo, 47
Bell, Gus, 139
Bench, John, 92
Bengough, Benny, 162
Berardino, Johnny, 109-110
Berg, Moe, 169
Bergman, Dave, 70-71, 196, 208, 215
Bergman, Steve, 70
Berra, Yogi, 131-133
Berry, Clair, 31
Blefary, Curt, 154
Bluejacket, Jim, 51-52
Blyzka, Mike, 78
Boggs, Wade, 37, 137, 139-142
Bolton, Tom, 88
Bonds, Barry, 203
Boone, Ray, 156
Bordetzki, Vincent, 104
Brady, Scott, 34
Brett, George, 135-137, 141, 189
Brewer, Billy, 178
Brickhouse, Jack, 14, 100
Bridges, Tommy, 112
Brief, Bunny, 104
Briggs, Walter, 31
Brinkman, Eddie, 66-67, 80

Brinkman, Joe, 38
Brock, Lou, 90-91
Brookens, Tom, 69
Broomfield, William, 14
Brown, Bobby, 165
Brown, Gates, 160, 181-182
Brown, Kevin, 185
Brucker, Earl, 138
Bunning, Jim, 215
Burch, Barney, 85
Burkett, Jesse, 105
Burns, Ed, 3
Burrell, Stanley, 115-116
Bush, George, 14, 209
Butsacaris, John, 207
Byrd, Harry, 78
Byrne, Charley, 183

C

Cambria, Joe, 39
Campanella, Roy, 97, 103
Campaneris, Bert, 209
Campbell, Bruce, 60
Campbell, James, 66, 93, 207
Carew, Rod, 190
Carey, Max, 16, 53-54
Carey, Nancy, 14
Carey, Patty 207
Carey, Paul, 14, 25, 207
Casey, Hugh, 113-115
Cash, Norman, 80, 154, 157, 158,
    209, 213
Cassell, Lou, 61
Castillo, Marty, 69
Castro, Fidel, 39
Catton, Bruce, 123

Chadwick, Henry, 41-42, 43
Chesbro, Jack, 185
Cicotte, Ed, 84
Cienscyk, Frank, 116
Clear, Bob, 95
Clemente, Roberto, 39
Cobb, Ty, 55, 58, 80-81, 91,
    119-120, 123-124, 134, 185
Colavito, Rocky, 37, 64, 149-150,
    159, 208
Coleman, Joe, 66, 80
Coleman, Ken, 22
Collins, Charles, 32-33
Collins, Eddie, 129
Collins, Pat, 161-162
Combs, Earle, 106, 161
Cowart, Dave, 35
Comiskey, Charles, 204
Craig, Roger, 186-187, 208
Cramer, Roger, 59
Crandall, Del, 211
Crawford, Sam, 190
Cronin, Joe, 59, 60, 200
Croucher, Frank, 60
Cuccinello, Tony, 103

D

Dapper, Cliff, 86
Darrow, Darrell, 95
Davis, Tommy, 12
Dean, Dizzy, 72-73
Del Guercio, Ted, 78
Demeter, Steve, 80
De Paul, St. Vincent, 145
Dennis, Patrick, 7
Dent, Bucky, 207, 213

Devens, Charlie, 122
Dewitt, Bill, 206
Dickey, Bill, 133, 162
Dickson, Paul, 111
Digby, Fred, 88
Dillon, Frank, 148
DiMaggio, Joe, 62, 142-143
Dingel, John, 14
Diroff, Joe, 208
DiSalvo, Pio, 34
Doan, Ray, 72
Dobronski, Carl, 35
Donatelli, Augie, 107-108
Dondero, Mike, 85
Downing, Al, 215
Dressen, Charlie, 37, 206
Dreyfuss, Barney, 152
Duffy, Frank, 79
Duffy, Hugh, 148
Dunn, Jack, 84
Duren, Ryne, 117-118
Durocher, Leo, 39, 55, 97-98,
    130-131, 168
Durst, Cedric, 79, 162
Dykes, Jimmy, 59, 77, 108

E

Eagan, Wish, 38, 39
Eason, Mal, 183
Ehlers, Arthur, 77
Eisenhower, Dwight, 110-111
Eliot, Sonny, 207
Engel, Bill, 98
Epstein, Mike, 155
Erskine, Carl, 113-114
Evans, Dwight, 33

Evans, Billy, 104-106
Evers, Walter (Hoot), 39

F

Falls, Joe, 171
Faust, Charles, 50-51
Feliciano, Jose, 207
Feller, Bob, 39, 147, 213
Feneck, Frank, 35-38
Fenton, Jack, 85
Ferrell, Rick, 206
Fetzer, John, 206
Fielder, Cecil, 35, 158, 207
Finley, Charles, 21, 52, 115-117,
    209
Finley, Chuck, 185
Firestone, Roy, 9
Fisk, Carlton, 96
Fleming, G.H., 203
Flick, Elmer, 80-81
Flood, Curt, 39, 213
Fonseca, Lew, 191
Ford, Ed (Whitey), 39, 157
Ford, Gerald, 27
Foreman, Lauren, 3
Fosse, Ray, 134
Foster, George, 79
Fox, Nelson, 150
Foxx, Jimmy, 32, 188-189
Franco, John, 187
Frazee, Harry, 84
Freehan, Bill, 66, 154, 159
Fridley, Jim, 78
Friend, Owen, 156
Frisch, Frank, 47-48, 107, 191
Fryman, Travis, 35, 203
Furillo, Carl, 97-98

G

Garagiola, Joe, 47, 132, 207
Garcia, Carlos, 203
Gaston, Cito, 200
Gazella, Mike, 161-162
Gehrig, Eleanor, 122
Gehrig, Lou, 32, 39, 122, 124, 161
Gehringer, Charlie, 31, 60, 207
Geishert, Vern, 79
George, Charlie (Greek), 85
Gibbs, Jake, 212
Gibson, Bob, 207, 213
Gibson, Kirk, 208, 215
Gilbert, Larry, 85
Ginsberg, Joe, 156
Girard, Joe, 161-162
Gladding, Fred, 155
Gomez, Ruben, 97
Gomez, Vernon (Lefty), 142
Gonzales, Mike, 169
Gonzalez, Juan, 203
Good, Matt, 35
Gosger, Jim, 212
Grabowski, 161-162
Grady, Mike, 49
Graham, Billy, 209
Grammas, Alex, 208
Graney, Jack, 191
Gray, Ted, 79
Greenberg, Hank, 31-33, 39, 207
Griffey, Ken Jr., 203
Griffin, Bob, 11-12
Grimm, Charlie, 17, 191
Grissom, Marquis, 203
Gromek, Steve, 155-156
Grove, Robert (Lefty), 32, 84, 128

H

Haak, Howie, 39
Hairston, Jerry, 214
Hammer, M.C., 116-117, 209
Hammond, Homer, 85
Haney, Larry, 154
Hanlon, Ned, 49
Hannan, Jim, 66, 80
Harrelson, Bud, 134
Harris, Earl, 156
Hartsfield, Roy, 87-88
Harwell, Davis, 4
Harwell, Julie, 14
Harwell, Lulu, 8, 14, 20
Hawley, Tony, 209
Hebner, Richie, 91, 172
Heilmann, Harry, 24-25, 191
Hein, Don, 25
Henneman, Mike, 159, 186
Herman, Alex, 72
Hernandez, Willie, 71, 159
Herrmann, Garry, 28-29
Heydler, John, 29, 152, 200
Higgins, Pinky, 2
Hiller, John, 159
Holloman, Bobo, 47-49
Homel, Jack, 206
Homer and Jethro, 209
Hornsby, Rogers, 3, 99-101, 125, 191
Horton, Willie, 40, 66, 154, 159, 212, 213
Hostetler, Chuck, 52-53
Houk, Ralph, 82-83
Houtteman, Art, 79, 156
Howlett, Grayle, 100

Hoyt, Waite, 98-99, 161
Hubbell, Carl, 189
Hudlin, Willis, 85
Hudson, Charles, 69
Huggins, Miller, 99, 106
Hughes, Roy, 53
Hunter, Billy, 78
Hunter, Herb, 122
Hutcheson, Joe, 53-54
Hutchinson, Fred, 155-156

I
Ilitch, Mike, 55-56
Irvin, Monte, 208

J
Jackson, Reggie, 170-171, 206
Jackson, Roy Lee, 71
Jeffcoat, Hal, 141
Jenkins, Ferguson, 92
Jennings, Hughie, 80, 163
Jimenez, Manny, 92
John, Tommy, 57, 60
Johnson, Ban, 29, 58
Johnson, Bob, 2
Johnson, Darrell, 78
Johnson, Walter, 128-129, 147, 191
Jones, Johnny, 84

K
Kaline, Al, 63, 66, 154, 157, 159, 181, 197, 207, 212
Kell, George, 24, 25, 149, 150, 205, 206
Keltner, Ken, 143

Kennedy, John F., 160
Kildee, Dale, 14
Killebrew, Harmon, 20, 64
King, Larry, 208
Kittle, Ron, 215
Klein, Chuck, 188-189
Kluszewski, Ted, 139
Kochivar, Tony, 36
Koufax, Sandy, 211, 212-213
Krichell, Paul, 39
Kryhoski, Dick, 78
Kuenn, Harvey, 62-64, 149
Kuralt, Charles, 207
Kile, Darryl, 203

L
Lajoie, Bill, 93
Landis, K.M., 28-30
Lane, Frank, 78
Lane, Ray, 11, 25, 149, 206
Larsen, Don, 77-78, 82
Lary, Frank, 150
Latham, Arlie, 40
Lazzeri, Tony, 5, 39, 161
Leibold, Nemo, 64-66
Lelivelt, Jack, 65
Lemon, Bob, 79
Lemon, Chet, 182
Leppert, Don, 78
Levin, Carl, 14
Lieb, Fred, 121-124
Limbaugh, Rush, 21
Lindstrom, Fred, 100
Littell, Mark, 136
Lockman, Shirley, 86
Lockman, Whitey, 44, 46, 86

Lofton, Ken, 203
Lolich, Mickey, 66, 159, 207
Lombardi, Ernie, 168
Lopez, Al, 126-128
Lopez, Aurelio, 69, 172
Lopez, Hector, 211
Lowe, John, 8
Lowenstein, John, 214
Lynn, Fred, 33

M

Mack, Connie, 59, 168, 189
Macklem, Leroy (Friday), 33
Maddox, Elliott, 66, 80
Maddux, Greg, 185
Maloney, Jim, 92
Mann, Earl, 85-86
Mantle, Mickey, 157
Marion, Marty, 48
Maris, Roger, 157
Marsh, Fred, 75
Martin, Billy, 37, 40, 209
Martin, Charles, 30-32
Martin, Mrs. Charles, 31
Martina, Joe, 85
Martinez, Buck, 171
Matthewson, Christy, 78-79
Mattick, Bob, 39
Mauch, Gene, 190
May, Lee, 182
Mays, Willie, 59, 130-131
McAuliffe, Dick, 60-61
McCatty, Steve, 116
McCarthy, J.P., 149
McCullough, Bill, 15-16
McCullough, Gladys, 16

McDaniel, Lindy, 212
McDonald, Jim, 78
McGill, Ralph, 3
McGraw, John, 40, 50-51, 169
McGuire, James T. (Deacon), 57-58
McLain, Denny, 66, 80, 117, 159,
    207, 212
McLaughlin, Ollie, 208
McNamara, John, 37, 208
McPhail, Larry, 5
McRae, Norm, 66, 80
Mead, William B., 111
Meany, Tom, 3, 100
Melvin, Bob, 69
Meoli, Rudi, 213
Merrill, Durwood, 208
Merta, Leo, 8
Meyer, Ray, 36
Mical, Bob, 35
Miller, Bill, 78
Miller, Dave, 93
Miller, Jon, 21-22
Miller, Todd, 9
Miller, Stu, 154
Miles, Clarence, 77
Middlesworth, Hal, 208
Miranda, Willie, 78
Mizell, Wilmer, 138
Molitor, Paul, 199-200
Montague, John, 214
Moon, Wally, 108
Moose, Ed, 9
Moran, Pat, 152
Moore, Euel, 85
Moore, Monte, 21-22
Moore, Wilcy, 162

Morehart, Ray, 161
Morris, Jack, 159, 215
Moses, Wally, 1-3
Mossi, Don, 157
Mowrey, Mike, 183
Mueller, Clarence (Heine) 81-82
Mullane, Tony, 58
Murray, Jim, 165
Musial, Stan, 98, 138, 208
Myers, Gene, 8

N

Narron, Sam, 107
Navin, Frank, 29, 30-31, 39, 80-81
Navin, Mrs. Frank, 30
Nelson, John, 35
Nemeth, Elsie, 208
Newhouse, Dave, 9
Newhouser, Hal, 39
Newsom, Bobo, 47
Nickle, Scott, 8, 9
Nicklin, Strande, 72
Nixon, Richard, 12
Northrup, Jim, 213

O

O'Dell, Bill, 211
Oglivie, Ben, 80
Oh, Sadaharu, 90
Olerud, John, 89-90, 203
Oliver, Al, 92
Oliver, Violet, 111-113
O'Neill, Steve, 53
Osborn, Gene, 25, 208
Ott, Mel, 25
Owen, Mickey, 113-114
Oyler, Ray, 61, 119, 154

P

Pafko, Andy, 87-88
Pagliarulo, Mike, 69
Paige, Leroy (Satchel), 71-75
Parrish, Lance, 69, 159, 209, 215
Parrott, Harold, 15-17
Patek, Fred, 92
Patrick, Van, 25
Paula, Carlos, 83
Peckinpaugh, Roger, 160
Pegler, Westbrook, 3
Pennock, Herb, 161-162
Perkins, Cy, 59
Petroskey, Dale, 12
Piazza, Mike, 203
Pierce, Billy, 39, 79
Pinson, Vada, 39
Pipp, Wally, 160
Plagenhoff, Vern, 12
Poffenberger, Cletus (Boots), 54-55
Post, Wally, 139
Povich, Maury, 20-21
Povich, Shirley, 20, 128-129
Pratt, Del, 160
Pruett, Hub, 124
Pytlak, Eric, 35

Q

Quinn, John, 87

R

Radbourn, Charles, 28
Raimi, Max, 208
Rathbun, Bob, 8, 25
Rather, Dan, 21
Redmond, Herbie, 208

Reichler, Joe, 78
Reagan, Ronald, 12-13, 209
Rice, Jim, 215
Rice, Grantland, 3
Richards, Paul, 6, 77, 171
Rickey, Branch, 16, 52, 81, 85-86
Riegle, Donald, 14
Righetti, Dave, 188
Rijo, Jose, 203
Ripley, Robert, 160
Rizzs, 8, 22-24, 25
Rizzuto, Phil, 39
Robertson, Orlo, 78
Robinson, Aaron, 79
Robinson, Brooks, 155, 208
Robinson, Frank, 39, 71, 137-139, 155
Robinson, Jackie, 11, 44
Rodriguez, Aurelio, 66, 80, 158-159
Roe, Rocky, 208
Rommel, Ed, 147
Roof, Gene, 8
Root, Charlie, 160
Rose, Pete, 66, 133-135, 170
Rowe, Lynwood (Schoolboy), 54
Rozman, Ronnie, 36
Ruel, Herold (Muddy), 128
Ruffing, Red, 79
Runyan, Damon, 3
Rusie, Amos, 78-79
Ruth, Claire, 122
Ruth, George (Babe), 3, 32, 84, 98-99, 106, 121-123, 134, 160-161
Ryan, Nolan, 57, 213

S
Sabatini, Len, 156
Salsinger, H.G., 3, 123
Sanguillen, Manny, 92
Schaal, Paul, 136
Schalk, Ray, 128
Scheffing, Bob, 19, 25, 47-48, 206
Schmakel, Jim, 33-35
Schmidt, Henry, 49-50
Schoendienst, Al (Red), 98
Schofield, Dick, 157
Segrist, Kal, 78
Selkirk, George, 202
Shaugnessy, Frank, 197
Shepard, Larry, 92
Shocker, Urban, 162
Short, Bob, 66
Shea, Gerald, 49
Shuba, George, 113-114
Skaff, Frank, 61
Skowron, Moose, 157
Simpson, Sarah, 209
Slapnicka, Cy, 39
Slaton, Jim, 80
Slayback, Bill, 207
Slayback, Robin, 207
Smith, Hal, 78
Smith, Jim, 51
Smith, John Francis, 183
Smith, John W., 119-120
Smith, Mayo, 37, 61
Smoltz, John, 93-94, 203
Spahn, Warren, 132
Speaker, Tris, 61-62
Spicer, Gary, 208
Spiller, Rell J., 68

Stallings, George, 148
Stanky, Ed, 107-108
Stanley, Mickey, 154
Stark, Dolly, 191
Staub, Rusty, 37
Stegman, Dave, 215
Stengel, Casey, 15-16
Stephens, Gene, 155
Stewart, Jimmy, 109
Stitzel, Howard, 24-25, 207

T

Tanana, Frank, 33, 94-96, 207, 208
Taylor, Tony, 208
Taylor, Zach, 74-75
Tebbetts, Birdie, 139
Temple, John, 139
Terrell, Walt, 208
Tettleton, Mickey, 35
Thomas, Frank, 203
Thomas, Myles, 162
Thompson, Denman, 3
Thomson, Bob, 45-46, 130-131
Torborg, Jeff, 186-188, 208
Torres, Mike, 213
Tracewski, Dick, 8, 69, 154, 211
Trammell, Alan, 34-35, 158, 208
Triandos, Gus, 78
Trout, Paul (Dizzy), 25, 39
Trucks, Virgil, 24
Tucker, Melody, 23
Turley, Bob, 77-78
Ty, Tyson, 5, 25

V

Valentine, Bobby, 37-38
Vaughn, Irving, 3

Veeck, Bill, 48
Virdon, Bill, 71

W

Walker, Jimmy, 147
Walker, Larry, 203
Waller, Bob, 21-22
Warner, Jack, 49
Wares, Clyde (Buzzy), 84
Washington, Herb, 52
Weaver, Earl, 6
Weaver, George (Buck), 64
Weik, Dick, 156
Weisman, Lefty, 105-106
Weiss, George, 77
Wera, Julie, 161-162
Wert, Don, 66, 80, 155, 159, 181, 212
Wertz, Vic, 24
Whitaker, Lou, 158, 195
White, Bill, 165
White, E.B., 151
Whitehill, Earl, 111-113
Wilcox, Milt, 214
Wilhelm, Hoyt, 86
Williams, Mitch, 118
Williams, Paul, 25
Williams, Ted, 124-126, 189
Willis, Vic, 185
Wills, Maury, 211-212
Wilson, Earl, 154, 155
Wilson, Glenn, 71
Wilson, Robert, 8
Winfield, Dave, 182, 189
Wockenfuss, John, 71
Wolff, Bob, 20

Wood, Jake, 154-155
Woodling, Gene, 78
Wyatt, Greg, 19-20

Y

Yastrzemski, Carl, 188, 214
Young, Cy, 84
Yount, Robin, 189

Z

Zeider, Rollie, 183
Zeller, Jack, 52